While every precaution has been taken in the preparation of this book, the publisher assumes no responsibility for errors or omissions, or for damages resulting from the use of the information contained herein.

FINANCIAL SECRETS OF THE 1%: REPAIR, REBUILD & RISE
INSIDER STRATEGIES TO RESTORE CREDIT, ACCESS CAPITAL & BUILD WEALTH FROM SCRATCH

First edition. November 3, 2025.

ISBN: 979-8231753864

Written by Keshia Davis.

AF687913

Table of Contents

Financial Secrets of the 1%: Repair, Rebuild & Rise Insider Strategies to Restore Credit, Access Capital & Build Wealth from Scratch

By:
Keshia Davis

Dedication

To every believer who has ever felt buried by debt, overlooked by systems, or silenced by financial shame—this book is for you.

To the warriors who rise early to pray, budget, and build, even when the breakthrough hasn't yet come. To the visionaries who dream of legacy while living paycheck to paycheck. To the mothers, fathers, entrepreneurs, and ministers who refuse to let lack define their future—you are seen, you are called, and you are equipped.

I dedicate this work to the remnant: Those who rebuild with broken bricks. Those who speak life over empty accounts. Those who sow in famine and reap in faith.

May every page restore your hope, sharpen your strategy, and ignite your authority. May you rise, rebuild, and reign—because Heaven has already approved your breakthrough.

With love, fire, and faith—this is for you.

Acknowledgements

To God be the glory—my Source, my Sustainer, and my Strategy. Every word in this book was birthed through prayer, warfare, and divine revelation. Thank You, Lord, for trusting me to steward this message and for breathing life into every chapter.

To my family, thank you for your unwavering support, your prayers, and your patience as I poured my heart into this work. Your love is my anchor, and your belief in me is my fuel.

To my spiritual mentors and prophetic intercessors—thank you for covering me, correcting me, and calling me higher. Your wisdom sharpened my voice, and your discernment protected my path.

To every reader, supporter, and Kingdom builder who has walked this journey with me—thank you for your hunger, your feedback, and your faith. You are the reason this book exists. May it empower you to rise, rebuild, and reign.

To the creative collaborators, editors, designers, and visionaries who helped shape this project—thank you for your excellence and your obedience. You didn't just contribute—you carried the mantle with me.

And finally, to the remnant—those who refuse to settle, who dare to believe, and who are ready to break every curse and build legacy through faith and strategy. This book is your blueprint. Thank you for saying yes to the call.

Introduction

Introduction: Breaking Financial Curses, Rebuilding Legacy, and Reigning in Kingdom Authority

This is not just a book—it's a battle plan. A prophetic blueprint for those who are ready to confront financial bondage, dismantle generational strongholds, and walk boldly into restoration, ownership, and legacy. Whether you've faced debt, denial, or delay, this resource was written to remind you: you are not powerless. You are positioned.

In these pages, you'll find more than financial advice. You'll discover Spirit-led strategies, biblical decrees, sample letters, trackers, and prayers that equip you to rise from ruin and rebuild with righteousness. You'll learn how to negotiate with creditors, challenge injustice, teach your children financial literacy, and activate generational wealth through credit, ownership, and stewardship.

This journey is for the remnant—the ones who refuse to settle for survival and are ready to reign. It's for the Kingdom entrepreneurs, the prophetic intercessors, the single parents, the community leaders, and the everyday believers who know that breakthrough is not just spiritual—it's practical.

Let this book be your companion in the trenches and your trumpet on the mountaintop. Let every chapter stir your faith, sharpen your strategy, and strengthen your voice. Because when faith and strategy collide, breakthrough is inevitable.

Welcome to your financial comeback. Welcome to your legacy. Welcome to your reign.

About the Author

Keshia Davis is a bold, visionary leader called to empower others through faith, strategy, and creative entrepreneurship. As the founder of *MidnightThreadz.shop* and *Batch & Bake*, she blends prophetic insight with practical tools to help believers rise from financial bondage and walk in legacy-building authority. Her work is rooted in spiritual warfare, financial literacy, and Kingdom impact—equipping readers to challenge injustice, rebuild what was broken, and reign with purpose.

Keshia is a hands-on creative director, financial educator, and mission architect. She crafts apparel that speaks like armor, writes resources that restore dignity, and builds brands that reflect divine identity. Her passion for justice and breakthrough is evident in every sample letter, prayer, and strategy she shares—each one designed to activate transformation and multiply impact.

Whether she's designing photorealistic mockups, writing prophetic declarations, or mentoring others in credit repair and ownership, Keshia leads with empathy, excellence, and fire. Her voice is one of clarity, conviction, and compassion—calling forth a generation of believers who are ready to rise, rebuild, and reign.

This book is not just her message—it's her mantle. And every page carries the sound of victory.

Part I: Decode the System - Breaking the Financial Matrix

The Veil Is About to Be Lifted

"For nothing is hidden that will not be made manifest, nor is anything secret that will not be known and come to light" (Luke 8:17).

For too long, the credit system has operated like a secret society—with hidden rules, coded language, and gatekeepers who profit from your confusion. Banks speak in algorithms while you're still trying to understand APR. Credit bureaus trade your data like commodities while you wonder why your score dropped. The wealthy leverage these systems for millions while you're denied a $5,000 car loan.

This isn't an accident. It's architecture. The system was built to be complex, to exhaust you into compliance, to make you feel too small to challenge it. But today, that changes. You're about to receive the decoder ring.

In Part I, you'll learn:

How credit scoring really works (not the kindergarten version)

Why banks reward debt and punish savers

How the 1% use credit as a wealth multiplier, not a survival tool

The psychological warfare designed to keep you borrowing

Why your credit report contains intentional errors (profit motive exposed)

How to read financial systems like the insiders do

"My people are destroyed for lack of knowledge" (Hosea 4:6). But not you. Not anymore. By the time you finish this section, you'll see the matrix. You'll understand why every "pre-approved" offer is a trap, why minimum payments are maximum slavery, and why the system needs you confused to stay profitable.

Knowledge isn't just power—it's freedom. And freedom is your birthright.

Chapter 1: The Credit Warfare System - How Banks Weaponize Your Score

Credit as a Weapon: The System Designed to Enslave

"The rich rule over the poor, and the borrower is slave to the lender" (Proverbs 22:7).

This scripture isn't just spiritual truth—it's the business model of modern banking. Credit wasn't created to help you; it was engineered to harvest your labor, monetize your dreams, and keep you perpetually one paycheck away from disaster. The credit system is a weapon, and most people don't even know they're in a war.

Here's how they weaponize your score: Access denial. Need an apartment? Credit check. Want that job? Credit check. Trying to get insurance? Credit check. Your FICO score has become your scarlet letter, following you everywhere, determining your worth in a system that profits from your struggle. They've turned a number into a noose.

The Psychology of the FICO Prison

"For as he thinks in his heart, so is he" (Proverbs 23:7).

The FICO score is psychological warfare masquerading as mathematics. Here's the sinister genius: They've convinced you that your score IS your identity. People say "I'm a 650" like they're confessing their worth as a human being. This is intentional.

The Three Psychological Weapons:

Shame: Bad credit becomes moral failure. You internalize the number until it shrinks your vision of what's possible. You stop applying, stop trying, stop believing.

Fear: They keep you terrified of your score dropping, so you make decisions from desperation instead of strategy. Fear makes you accept 29% interest rates because "at least someone approved me."

Addiction: Good credit feels like validation. You chase the high of approval, taking on debt you don't need just to see the number rise. *"All things are lawful for me, but I will not be brought under the power of any" (1 Corinthians 6:12).*

Why Banks Reward Debt: The Profit Matrix Exposed

Here's the truth that will set you free: Banks don't make money from people who pay off their balances. They call us "deadbeats"—literally. Their ideal customer carries a balance, pays interest forever, and never quite escapes.

"No one can serve two masters. Either you will hate the one and love the other, or you will be devoted to the one and despise the other. You cannot serve both God and money" (Matthew 6:24).

The system rewards debt because:

Interest payments are pure profit (they created money from nothing)

Minimum payments ensure 20+ years of servitude

Late fees generate $12 billion annually

Over-limit fees add another $1 billion

They WANT you in debt. Your struggle is their business model. Your bondage is their bonus structure.

Flipping the Script: Using Their Weapons Against Them

"I am sending you out like sheep among wolves. Therefore be as shrewd as snakes and as innocent as doves" (Matthew 10:16).

It's time to flip their own system against them. Here's how to turn their weapons into your tools:

1. Leverage Their Greed Banks compete viciously for profitable customers. Use this. Apply for multiple cards when your score hits 700+, rack up sign-up bonuses, then pay in full. You just made $2,000 from their desperation.

2. Weaponize the Grace Period Every credit card has a 21-25 day grace period. Use their money interest-free for three weeks, earn rewards, pay in full. You're now profiting from the same system designed to enslave.

3. Manufacture Perfect History Set up automatic payments for tiny amounts. $5 Netflix on five different cards = 60 positive payment records per year. You're using their own reporting system to build an impeccable profile.

4. Use Debt as a Tool, Not a Crutch *"The plans of the diligent lead to profit as surely as haste leads to poverty" (Proverbs 21:5).*

Borrow only for appreciating assets

Never finance depreciating items

Use 0% offers to keep YOUR money invested

The Kingdom Credit Mindset

The world's system says your worth equals your score. The Kingdom says your worth was settled at Calvary. But wisdom says use the world's system to fund Kingdom purposes.

"And if you have not been trustworthy with someone else's property, who will give you property of your own?" (Luke 16:12). Credit is "someone else's property"—the bank's money. Prove faithful with it, and God will trust you with true riches.

Your New Credit Warfare Strategy:

See credit as a tool, not an identity

Use their money to make money

Never pay interest unless it builds wealth

Let perfect payments preach your testimony

Build credit to bless others, not impress others

Remember: The same Jesus who flipped tables in the temple would flip the credit system to advance His Kingdom. Be angry at the system, not enslaved by it. Use it, don't let it use you.

"You intended to harm me, but God intended it for good to accomplish what is now being done, the saving of many lives" (Genesis 50:20). What the enemy meant for bondage, God can use for breakthrough. Your credit score is about to become your testimony.

***

Section 1: How the Credit System Really Works

What the 1% Understand About Credit Scoring, Utilization, and Leverage

Here's the truth the wealthy don't want you to know: Credit isn't just about getting approved—it's about accessing the same leverage tools that build empires. When Amazon needs cash, they don't sell their stocks. They borrow against them at rates so low it's practically free money. The difference between you and Jeff Bezos isn't just zeros in the bank account—it's understanding how to make your assets work *for* you instead of sitting idle.

How Corporations Like Amazon Use Leverage

Amazon maintains a debt-to-equity ratio of just 0.24 (as of 2024), meaning they borrow strategically while keeping massive equity. But here's the genius part: They don't borrow because they *need* money—they borrow because it's cheaper than using their own cash. When you can borrow at 3-4% and invest that money for 10-15% returns, you're literally creating wealth from thin air. This is called positive arbitrage, and it's how the wealthy stay wealthy.

How Regular Consumers Can Play the Same Game

You might not have Amazon's balance sheet, but you have more leverage options than you realize:

1. Securities-Based Lending (Your Stock Portfolio as an ATM)

Borrow up to 50-70% of your portfolio's value

Interest rates as low as 2-5% (way better than credit cards)

Keep your stocks growing while accessing cash

No credit check required—your stocks ARE the credit

2. Margin Accounts (The Double-Edged Sword)

Borrow up to 50% of your stock value to buy more stocks

Can amplify gains (and losses)

Best for experienced investors who understand the risks

Start small—practice with 10-20% leverage first

3. 401(k) Loans (Borrowing from Your Future Self)

Borrow up to $50,000 or 50% of your balance

Pay yourself back with interest (usually 5-6%)

No credit check, no taxes if repaid on time

Downside: You miss market gains on borrowed amount

4. Home Equity Lines of Credit (Your House as a Bank)

Access 80-90% of your home's equity

Rates typically 1-3% above prime

Interest may be tax-deductible

Use for investments, not consumption

5. Whole Life Insurance Loans (The Secret Weapon)

Borrow against cash value at 4-6% interest

Your policy keeps growing as if you never borrowed

No credit check, flexible repayment

The wealthy call this "infinite banking"

6. Business Credit Lines (Think Like a CEO)

Get an EIN (it's free) and build business credit

Access lines of credit separate from personal credit

Can leverage business assets you don't even own yet

Start with secured business cards, graduate to unsecured lines

The Golden Rules of Leverage

Never borrow to consume—only to invest or produce income

Keep your leverage under 30% of total assets

Have 6-12 months of payments in reserve

Understand margin calls—markets go down too

Start small—practice with $1,000 before risking $10,000

Real-World Example

Sarah has $50,000 in stocks and a paid-off car worth $20,000. Instead of selling stocks (triggering taxes) to start her business, she:

Takes a securities-based loan for $25,000 at 4% interest

Keeps her stocks growing at historical 10% average

Deducts business loan interest from taxes

Nets 6% profit just from the arbitrage

This is how the wealthy think—not "Can I afford it?" but "What's the smartest way to access capital?"

Remember: The credit system isn't designed to help you survive—it's designed to help banks profit. But when you understand the rules, you can play the game just like the 1% do. The key is using credit as a tool for building wealth, not as a crutch for consumption.

***

Section 2: The Secured Loan Strategy & Common Credit Pitfalls

Building Credit with Your Own Money: The Bank's Best-Kept Secret

"The rich rule over the poor, and the borrower is slave to the lender." - Proverbs 22:7

But what if you could flip this scripture on its head? What if you became both the lender AND the borrower, using wisdom to build wealth instead of bondage?

Here's a strategy the wealthy use that banks don't advertise: **secured credit building**. You're about to learn how to use your own money to manufacture a perfect payment history, boost your credit score by 50-100 points, and position yourself for real funding—all while keeping your cash safe.

The $20,000 Credit Building Blueprint

This strategy is so simple it feels like cheating, but it's completely legal and incredibly effective:

1. **Deposit Your Seed Money** Take $20,000-$30,000 and put it in a savings account or CD at your bank. This becomes your collateral. *"Whoever can be trusted with very little can also be trusted with much" (Luke 16:10).* You're proving to the bank—and yourself—that you can handle money wisely.
2. **Request a Secured Loan** Ask the bank for a loan against your deposit. They'll typically lend you 90-100% of your deposited amount at a low interest rate (usually 2-4% above what your savings earns). The bank loves this—zero risk for them.
3. **Let the Money Work** Here's where discipline matters: Take the loan proceeds and put them in a separate high-yield savings account. DO NOT SPEND IT. This isn't play money—it's credit-building capital. *"The plans of the diligent lead to profit as surely as haste leads to poverty" (Proverbs 21:5).*
4. **Make Perfect Payments for Six Months** Set up automatic payments from the loan proceeds account. Every on-time payment

adds positive history to your credit report. Three bureaus × six months = 18 positive marks on your credit.

5. **Pay It Off and Repeat** After six months, pay off the remaining balance. Your credit score just jumped, you still have most of your money, and you've built a relationship with the bank. Now you can qualify for unsecured credit at better rates.

The Hidden Benefits No One Talks About

- **Credit Mix Improvement**: Adds an installment loan to your profile (10% of your FICO score)
- **Payment History**: Creates 6-12 months of perfect payments (35% of your FICO score)
- **Banking Relationship**: Establishes you as a "preferred customer" for future loans
- **Psychological Win**: Builds your confidence in managing larger amounts
- **Interest Arbitrage**: If you use a high-yield savings account, you offset some interest costs

The 7 Deadly Credit Sins Most Consumers Commit

"My people are destroyed for lack of knowledge" (Hosea 4:6). Here are the mistakes keeping you in financial bondage:

1. Paying Only Minimums The minimum payment is designed to keep you in debt for decades. Always pay at least double the minimum. *"Let no debt remain outstanding, except the continuing debt to love one another" (Romans 13:8).*

2. Closing Old Credit Cards Length of credit history is 15% of your score. That old card you got at 18? Keep it open with a small recurring charge like Netflix.

3. Applying for Too Much Credit at Once Each hard inquiry can drop your score 5-10 points. Space applications 6 months apart. *"Patient planning brings profit; hasty speculation brings poverty" (Proverbs 21:5, TLB).*

4. Ignoring Credit Reports 25% of reports have errors. Check all three bureaus quarterly. Dispute everything that's not 100% accurate. The burden of proof is on them, not you.

5. Maxing Out Credit Cards Keep utilization under 30% per card and under 10% overall. The wealthy use credit for convenience, not survival.

6. Paying Late "Just Once" One 30-day late payment can drop your score 100 points and stay on your report for 7 years. Set up autopay for at least minimums. *"Let your 'Yes' be 'Yes,' and your 'No,' 'No'" (Matthew 5:37).*

7. Not Understanding the Game Credit scoring is a game with specific rules. Learn them. Master them. Win.

The Borrowing Mindset Shift

Most people borrow from desperation. The wealthy borrow from strategy. Here's the kingdom perspective:

- **Poor Mindset**: "I need money, so I'll borrow"
- **Wealthy Mindset**: "I'll borrow to build credit and relationships for future opportunities"
- **Kingdom Mindset**: "I'll use the world's system to fund God's purposes"

"I tell you, use worldly wealth to gain friends for yourselves, so that when it is gone, you will be welcomed into eternal dwellings" (Luke 16:9). Jesus literally told us to be strategic with money!

Your 90-Day Credit Transformation Action Plan

1. **Week 1-2**: Pull all three credit reports, dispute errors
2. **Week 3-4**: Open high-yield savings, gather your seed money
3. **Week 5-6**: Apply for secured loan, set up automatic payments
4. **Month 2-3**: Monitor credit weekly, pay all bills early
5. **Month 3**: Apply for one strategic credit card with rewards
6. **Ongoing**: Never miss a payment, keep utilization low, build relationships

Remember: *"In their hearts humans plan their course, but the Lord establishes their steps" (Proverbs 16:9).* Commit your credit rebuilding to

God, use these strategies with integrity, and watch Him open doors that no FICO score can shut.

Your credit score isn't your identity—but it can be your tool for Kingdom impact. Master it. Don't let it master you.

***

Section 3: The Phantom Credit Strategy & Alternative Payment Reporting

Building Credit Without Spending: The Discipline of Financial Fasting

"But the fruit of the Spirit is love, joy, peace, forbearance, kindness, goodness, faithfulness, gentleness and self-control" (Galatians 5:22-23).

Self-control isn't just a spiritual virtue—it's a wealth-building superpower. What if I told you that the fastest way to build credit is to get approved for it... then pretend it doesn't exist?

The Zero-Spend Credit Building Method

Here's what the credit card companies pray you never figure out: **They make nothing from responsible users.** When you get approved for credit lines but never use them, you become their worst nightmare and your credit score's best friend.

The Strategy:

1. Apply for 2-3 credit cards with no annual fees
2. Get approved for the highest limits possible
3. Put the cards in a drawer (or literally freeze them in ice)
4. Never spend a single dollar
5. Watch your score climb 50-100 points in 90 days

"Whoever has no rule over his own spirit is like a city broken down, without walls" (Proverbs 25:28). Those pieces of plastic are testing your walls. Pass the test.

Why This Works: The Mathematics of Restraint

Your credit utilization ratio accounts for 30% of your FICO score. Here's the beautiful math:

- **Before**: $5,000 in debt on $10,000 limit = 50% utilization (poor)
- **After adding unused cards**: $5,000 debt on $25,000 limit = 20% utilization (good)
- **Best case**: $0 debt on $25,000 limit = 0% utilization (excellent)

You just improved your score without spending OR paying down a penny. *"The wise store up choice food and olive oil, but fools gulp theirs down" (Proverbs 21:20).*

The Secret Weapon: Alternative Payment Reporting

While you're building phantom credit, there's gold hiding in your everyday bills. The average person makes 12+ on-time payments monthly that never touch their credit report. It's time to change that.

Rent Reporting Services:

- **RentTrack**: Reports to all 3 bureaus for $9.95/month
- **Piñata**: Free reporting plus rewards for on-time payment
- **PaymentReport**: $10/month, includes back-reporting up to 2 years
- **Boom**: Reports rent, utilities, and streaming services

Utility & Bill Reporting:

- **Experian Boost**: Free, adds utilities, phone, streaming (average 13-point increase)
- **eCredable**: Reports utilities to TransUnion
- **LevelCredit**: Reports rent and utilities for $6.95/month

"Let no debt remain outstanding, except the continuing debt to love one another" (Romans 13:8). You're already paying these bills faithfully—now let them testify on your behalf!

The Phone Bill Credit Hack

Your cell phone bill is a goldmine of credit-building potential:

1. **Switch to Postpaid**: Prepaid doesn't build credit; postpaid does
2. **Add to Experian Boost**: Instant history, instant points
3. **Finance a Phone**: 0% APR installment = positive payment history
4. **Never Miss**: Set autopay 3 days before due date

One woman added 24 months of perfect T-Mobile payments to her report and gained 47 points overnight. *"Many will say to me on that day, 'Lord, Lord'... Then I will tell them plainly, 'I never knew you'" (Matthew*

7:22-23). Make sure your credit report "knows" all your good payment behavior!

The Biblical Balance: When to Use Credit

Not using credit cards doesn't mean never using them. Here's kingdom wisdom:

Use Credit For:

- Recurring bills (then autopay from checking)
- Gas once a month (builds history)
- Emergencies (true ones, not shoe sales)

Never Use Credit For:

- Emotional purchases
- Things you can't afford
- Impressing people (*"Do not wear yourself out to get rich; do not trust your own cleverness" - Proverbs 23:4*)

The 0% Utilization Myth Buster

Credit bureaus want to see you CAN use credit responsibly, not that you're afraid of it. Keep 1-3% utilization on one card:

- $3 Netflix subscription on a $1,000 limit card = 0.3% utilization
- Autopay the full balance
- Perfect score formula achieved

Your "Ghost Credit" Implementation Plan

Month 1:

- Apply for 2 no-fee cards (spread applications by 2 weeks)
- Sign up for Experian Boost
- Add rent to credit report via free service

Month 2:

- Receive cards, activate, then lock in safe

- Put one tiny recurring charge on one card
- Add all utilities to credit reporting

Month 3:

- Check scores (expect 30-50 point jump)
- Apply for one more card if score above 650
- Celebrate without spending!

"For which of you, desiring to build a tower, does not first sit down and count the cost?" (Luke 14:28). The cost of building credit isn't money—it's discipline.

The Testimony Hidden in Your Score

Every point your score increases is a testimony to faithfulness. Every on-time payment preaches a sermon about integrity. Your credit report is becoming your financial resume, and restraint is writing the best references.

Remember: The same Holy Spirit that gives you power over sin gives you power over spending. *"I can do all things through Christ who strengthens me" (Philippians 4:13)*—including leaving credit cards untouched and letting your everyday faithfulness build kingdom wealth.

Your credit score is about to increase not because you spent more, but because you mastered more. That's kingdom economics—multiplication through restraint, increase through discipline, blessing through obedience.

***

Section 4: The 1% Credit Code - What the Wealthy Know That You Don't

The Million-Dollar Mindset Shift

"For My thoughts are not your thoughts, neither are your ways My ways," declares the Lord. "As the heavens are higher than the earth, so are My ways higher than your ways and My thoughts than your thoughts" (Isaiah 55:8-9).

The wealthy don't think about credit the way you've been taught to think about it. While you're worried about approval, they're calculating leverage. While you're avoiding debt, they're strategically deploying it. The 1% understand a secret: **Credit isn't about borrowing money—it's about borrowing opportunity.**

The Three Pillars of Wealth-Building Credit

1. Credit as Currency, Not Crutch

The wealthy never use credit for consumption—only for production. They understand that every dollar borrowed at 4% that generates 12% return creates an 8% profit from thin air. *"Well done, good and faithful servant! You have been faithful with a few things; I will put you in charge of many things" (Matthew 25:21).* They multiply borrowed money like the servants multiplied talents.

Example: A wealthy investor borrows $500,000 at 4% to buy rental properties yielding 11%. That's $35,000 annual profit using the bank's money. You could do this with $50,000 or even $5,000—the principle scales.

2. Utilization Is a Game, Not a Grade

While you're keeping one card at 30%, the wealthy have 20 cards at 1%. They understand the algorithm: Total available credit matters more than individual card usage. They'll have $500,000 in available credit while using $5,000. That's 1% utilization—credit score gold.

"The wisdom of the prudent is to give thought to their ways, but the folly of fools is deception" (Proverbs 14:8). They've thought through the system and discovered: More accounts with tiny balances beats fewer accounts with higher usage.

3. Leverage Is a Lever, Not a Liability

The wealthy use credit like a crowbar—to move mountains they couldn't budge with cash alone. They understand timing: Borrow when rates are low, invest when opportunities are high, repay when assets appreciate.

The 1% Credit Commandments

First Commandment: Never Let Credit Sit Idle Every credit line is a sleeping soldier. The wealthy activate them strategically:

- Business credit funds inventory that sells for 3x cost
- Personal credit captures limited-time investment opportunities
- Real estate lines fund flips that profit $30,000 in 90 days

"Whoever watches the wind will not plant; whoever looks at the clouds will not reap" (Ecclesiastes 11:4). They act while others analyze.

Second Commandment: Build Relationships, Not Just Reports The 1% know their banker's children's names. They golf with the branch manager. When opportunity knocks, their loan is approved over lunch, not through an algorithm. *"A gift opens the way and ushers the giver into the presence of the great" (Proverbs 18:16).*

Third Commandment: Create Credit Entities Why have one credit profile when you can have five? The wealthy build credit through:

- Personal name
- Business EIN
- Trust structures
- Investment LLCs
- Holding companies

Each entity can borrow separately. Five entities with $100,000 credit each = $500,000 in leverage opportunity.

The Secret Sauce: Velocity Banking

Here's what will blow your mind—the wealthy pay off 30-year mortgages in 5-7 years using credit cards. It's called velocity banking:

1. Get a HELOC or high-limit card
2. Pay chunks of mortgage principal

3. Use mortgage payment savings to pay off the credit line
4. Repeat until mortgage is gone (Refer to Section 5 of Ch.1)

"The borrower is slave to the lender" (Proverbs 22:7)—so they become free as fast as possible.

The Utilization Matrix Decoded

What you learned: Keep credit utilization under 30% What the 1% know: Keep it under 10% aggregate, under 5% per card

Here's their blueprint:

- 20+ credit cards (yes, twenty)
- $300,000+ total credit limit
- $3,000 total usage
- 1% utilization = 800+ credit score

They're not credit card collectors—they're credit score architects.

The Leverage Lifestyle

The wealthy live by this principle: **Use credit for assets, cash for liabilities.**

- Buying real estate? Credit.
- Buying a business? Credit.
- Buying dinner? Cash.
- Buying clothes? Cash.

"She considers a field and buys it; out of her earnings she plants a vineyard" (Proverbs 31:16). Notice—she considers (strategy), buys (investment), and plants (multiplication). That's the 1% way.

Your Wealth-Building Credit Action Plan

1. **Shift Your Mindset**: Credit is a wealth-building tool, not a survival mechanism
2. **Multiply Your Accounts**: Apply for a new card every 6 months once you're over 720
3. **Lower Your Utilization**: Add credit lines, don't add spending

4. **Build Banking Relationships**: Bank where you want to borrow
5. **Think Business**: Get an EIN and build a second credit profile
6. **Deploy Strategically**: Only borrow for things that make money

Remember: *"I have come that they may have life, and have it to the full" (John 10:10).* God doesn't want you surviving on credit—He wants you thriving with it. The 1% understand this. Now you do too.

Your credit score isn't your ceiling—it's your catapult. Use it like the wealthy do: strategically, purposefully, and profitably. The same God who multiplied loaves and fishes can multiply your credit into kingdom wealth. But first, you must think like the 1%, not the 99%.

***

Section 5: Real-World Velocity Banking Example: Sarah's 30-Year Mortgage Freedom in 6 Years

The Setup: Sarah's Financial Snapshot

Sarah owns a $300,000 home with a $240,000 mortgage at 6% interest. Her monthly payment is $1,439 (principal + interest). After 5 years of payments, she still owes $222,000 and has barely dented the principal. At this rate, she'll pay $278,000 in interest over 30 years. She's sick of being enslaved to the bank.

"The borrower is slave to the lender" (Proverbs 22:7). Sarah decides: No more slavery.

Step 1: Sarah Gets Her Velocity Banking Tools

- Opens a HELOC (Home Equity Line of Credit) for $50,000 at 7% interest
- Gets a high-limit credit card with $20,000 limit at 0% for 18 months
- Monthly take-home income: $6,000
- Monthly expenses: $4,000 (including mortgage)
- Monthly cash flow: $2,000

Step 2: The First Velocity Strike
Month 1:

- Sarah puts her entire $6,000 income into the HELOC
- Uses HELOC to pay all expenses ($4,000)
- Takes $10,000 from HELOC and makes a principal-only payment on mortgage
- New mortgage balance: $212,000 (just saved $45,000 in interest!)
- HELOC balance: $8,000 ($10,000 principal payment - $2,000 cash flow)

Step 3: The Compound Effect

Months 2-5:

- Continues depositing all income into HELOC
- Pays all expenses from HELOC
- Each month, HELOC balance drops by $2,000 (her cash flow)
- Month 5: HELOC balance is $0

Month 6:

- Repeats the cycle—another $10,000 principal payment
- Mortgage balance drops to $202,000

The Acceleration Secret
Here's where it gets beautiful. Each $10,000 principal payment:

- Saves approximately $18,000 in interest (at 6% over remaining years)
- Reduces the loan term by 3-4 years
- Costs only $300-400 in HELOC interest (paid off in 5 months)

The Math That Sets You Free:

- Traditional method: $278,000 total interest over 30 years
- Velocity banking: $42,000 total interest over 6 years
- Total savings: $236,000
- Time saved: 24 years of payments

Year-by-Year Breakdown
Year 1: 2 cycles = $20,000 principal reduction
Year 2: 2.4 cycles = $24,000 principal reduction
Year 3: 2.4 cycles = $24,000 principal reduction
Year 4: 2.4 cycles = $24,000 principal reduction
Year 5: 2.4 cycles = $24,000 principal reduction
Year 6: Final payoff = $106,000 remaining

By year 6, Sarah can use her HELOC one final time, combined with savings, to eliminate the mortgage entirely.

The Credit Card Amplifier

For even faster results, Sarah uses her 0% credit card:

- Pays $20,000 mortgage principal with 0% card
- Uses monthly cash flow to pay off card over 10 months
- Zero interest cost, massive interest savings
- Repeats when new 0% offers arrive

Critical Success Factors

This ONLY works if:

1. You have positive monthly cash flow
2. You're disciplined (no new debt)
3. Your HELOC rate is reasonable
4. You pay expenses from HELOC, not separate accounts
5. You understand it's YOUR money cycling through

Warning Signs to Stop:

- Cash flow turns negative
- HELOC rate exceeds mortgage rate by 3%+
- You're tempted to spend the available credit
- Job stability becomes questionable

The Kingdom Perspective

"Suppose one of you wants to build a tower. Won't you first sit down and estimate the cost to see if you have enough money to complete it?" (Luke 14:28)

Sarah counted the cost:

- Traditional path: 30 years of bondage, $518,000 total paid
- Velocity path: 6 years of strategy, $282,000 total paid
- Freedom gained: 24 years and $236,000

This isn't about getting rich—it's about getting free. Free to give, free to serve, free to pursue God's calling without a mortgage chain around your neck.

Remember: Velocity banking is a tool, not a toy. It requires discipline, cash flow, and careful execution. But for those who master it, it's the difference between 30 years of slavery and 6 years of strategic freedom. The wealthy do this quietly while the masses make minimum payments. Now you know their secret.

"My people are destroyed for lack of knowledge" (Hosea 4:6). Not anymore. Not you. Not today.

***

Section 6: The Early Payment Advantage - Why Timing Is Everything "Credit Cards"

The Due Date Deception

"The prudent see danger and take refuge, but the simple keep going and pay the penalty" (Proverbs 27:12).

Here's what the **credit card** companies don't advertise: Your due date is already too late. By the time your due date arrives, your balance has already been reported to the credit bureaus, your utilization has been calculated, and your credit score has been impacted. The wealthy know this. The masses don't.

Most people celebrate paying "on time" while their credit scores suffer from high utilization they could have avoided. The game isn't about paying on time—it's about paying at the RIGHT time.

The Statement Date Secret

Every credit card has two critical dates:

- **Statement Date**: When your balance is snapshot and reported to bureaus
- **Due Date**: When payment is required (usually 21-25 days after statement date)

Here's the wealth-building hack: **Pay BEFORE your statement date, not just before your due date.**

"The plans of the diligent lead to profit as surely as haste leads to poverty" (Proverbs 21:5). The diligent plan their payments; the hasty react to due dates.

Example: Sarah has a $5,000 limit card with a $2,500 balance.

- If she pays on the **due date**: 50% utilization reported (hurts score)
- If she pays before **statement date**: 0% utilization reported (helps score)
- Same payment, different timing, 50-point score difference

The 15/3 Payment Method of the Wealthy

The 1% use what insiders call the "15/3 Method":

1. Pay half your balance 15 days before due date
2. Pay remaining balance 3 days before due date

This achieves three powerful results:

- Keeps reported balance near zero
- Shows multiple payments per month (banks love activity)
- Prevents any chance of late payment

"In the morning sow your seed, and at evening withhold not your hand, for you do not know which will prosper, this or that, or whether both alike will be good" (Ecclesiastes 11:6). Multiple payments create multiple opportunities for credit building.

The Psychological Warfare of Being Ahead

When you pay after the statement date, you're always behind. When you pay before, you're always ahead. This shift changes everything:

Behind Mindset: Stressed, reactive, fearful of missing payments **Ahead Mindset**: Peaceful, strategic, confident in your system

"Therefore do not worry about tomorrow, for tomorrow will worry about itself" (Matthew 6:34). When you pay early, tomorrow's payment is already handled.

The Credit Score Multiplication Effect

Here's what happens when you pay before statement dates:

- Month 1: 0% utilization reported instead of 30% = +25 points
- Month 3: Pattern established = +15 more points
- Month 6: "Excellent payment behavior" = +20 more points
- Total gain: 60 points just from payment timing

The Advanced Early Payment Strategy

Level 1: Pay in full before statement date **Level 2**: Make multiple payments throughout the month **Level 3**: Pay immediately after each purchase

The wealthy often treat credit cards like debit cards—charging and paying within 24-48 hours. This creates:

- Zero balance reporting
- Maximum payment history
- Complete interest avoidance
- Psychological freedom from debt

"Owe no one anything except to love each other" (Romans 13:8). When you pay immediately, you truly owe no one.

Your Early Payment Implementation Plan

1. **Find Your Statement Date**: Call or check online (usually same day monthly)
2. **Set Reminders**: 5 days before statement date
3. **Pay to Zero**: Or keep under 3% for optimal scoring
4. **Track Results**: Watch your score jump within 30-60 days
5. **Automate**: Set auto-pay for 3 days before statement date

The Kingdom Perspective on Being Early

"The soul of the sluggard craves and gets nothing, while the soul of the diligent is richly supplied" (Proverbs 13:4).

Paying early isn't just about credit scores—it's about character. It demonstrates:

- Diligence over procrastination
- Wisdom over minimum compliance
- Freedom over bondage
- Excellence over mediocrity

When you pay early, you're declaring: "I am not a slave to this system. I am a strategic steward of the resources God has entrusted to me."

Remember: The same God who commands us to "seek first the Kingdom" (Matthew 6:33) honors those who put first things first in every area—including credit card payments. The early payer gets the points, the peace, and the power to build wealth instead of managing debt.

Your new motto: Pay before they ask, and watch your score soar.

Chapter 2: How to Read & Clean Your Credit Report Like a Pro

Breaking the Code: Your Credit Report Demystified

"My people are destroyed for lack of knowledge; because you have rejected knowledge, I reject you from being a priest for me" (Hosea 4:6).

Your credit report isn't just numbers and codes—it's a testimony written in financial language. Every line tells a story about your faithfulness, your struggles, and your victories. But if you can't read it, you can't rewrite it. Today, we decode the mystery and give you the keys to your financial freedom.

Pulling Your Report: Your Legal Right to Financial Truth

You have a God-given and government-protected right to see exactly what lenders see. The Fair Credit Reporting Act guarantees you free access to all three credit reports annually. Here's how to claim what's yours:

The Only Legitimate Source: AnnualCreditReport.com

- Not the singing commercials sites (they charge fees)
- Not the "free trial" traps
- The official government-mandated portal

Pull All Three—They're Different:

- **Equifax**: Often shows mortgage/real estate history best
- **Experian**: Usually most comprehensive for credit cards
- **TransUnion**: Sometimes has accounts others miss

"Test all things; hold fast what is good" (1 Thessalonians 5:21). Test all three bureaus—don't assume they match.

The 5 Sacred Factors That Control Your Score

Understanding these five factors is like having the blueprint to the temple. Master them, and you master your financial destiny:

1. Payment History (35%)—Your Faithfulness Score *"Let your 'Yes' be 'Yes,' and your 'No,' 'No'" (Matthew 5:37).*

- Every payment is a promise kept or broken
- One 30-day late can drop your score 100 points
- Seven years of consequences for one month of struggle
- Strategy: Automate minimums, pay in full manually

2. Credit Utilization (30%)—Your Restraint Score *"Like a city whose walls are broken through is a person who lacks self-control" (Proverbs 25:28).*

- The percentage of available credit you're using
- Under 10% = Excellent | Under 30% = Good | Over 50% = Danger
- Calculated per card AND overall
- Strategy: Ask for limit increases, not spending increases

3. Length of Credit History (15%)—Your Maturity Score *"Remember the days of old; consider the generations long past" (Deuteronomy 32:7).*

- Average age of all accounts matters
- Never close your oldest card (it's your credit cornerstone)
- New accounts lower average age temporarily
- Strategy: Keep old accounts active with small charges

4. Credit Mix (10%)—Your Diversity Score *"Two are better than one, because they have a good return for their labor" (Ecclesiastes 4:9).*

- Variety shows sophistication: cards, installment loans, mortgage
- Don't need all types, but monotony hurts
- Strategy: Add a small personal loan or car loan when strategic

5. New Credit (10%)—Your Desperation Score *"The prudent see danger and take refuge, but the simple keep going and pay the penalty" (Proverbs 27:12).*

- Multiple applications signal financial distress
- Each hard inquiry can cost 5-10 points
- Inquiries fade after 12 months, disappear after 24
- Strategy: Space applications 6+ months apart

Spotting Errors: The Hidden Thieves in Your Report

Studies show 79% of credit reports contain errors. That's 4 out of 5 people being robbed by mistakes. Here's your detection guide:

Common Errors That Steal Points:

- Accounts that aren't yours (identity theft or mixed files)
- Paid accounts showing as unpaid
- Duplicate accounts (same debt listed twice)
- Wrong credit limits (makes utilization look worse)
- Incorrect late payments
- Accounts older than 7 years still reporting

Red Flags of Identity Theft:

- Addresses you've never lived at
- Employers you've never worked for
- Inquiries from companies you don't recognize
- Accounts opened when you were a minor

"The thief comes only to steal and kill and destroy; I have come that they may have life, and have it to the full" (John 10:10). Don't let errors steal your financial life.

The Professional's Clean-Up Strategy

Step 1: Document Everything

- Print all three reports
- Highlight every error in different colors
- Create a spreadsheet tracking each dispute

Step 2: Gather Your Evidence

- Payment receipts
- Account statements
- Court documents
- Identity documents

Step 3: Dispute Like a Lawyer

- Write separate letters for each bureau
- One issue per letter (don't overwhelm)
- Send certified mail, return receipt requested
- Keep copies of everything

Sample Dispute Language: "I am formally disputing the following inaccurate information on my credit report. Under the Fair Credit Reporting Act, you have 30 days to investigate and correct or remove this information. [Specific account details]. This information is inaccurate because [specific reason]. Attached is documentation proving [your claim]."

Your 30-Day Credit Report Transformation Plan

Week 1: Pull all three reports, identify all errors **Week 2**: Gather documentation, write dispute letters **Week 3**: Mail disputes, start payment optimization **Week 4**: Follow up, document responses, plan next moves

Remember: *"Write the vision and make it plain on tablets, that he may run who reads it" (Habakkuk 2:2).* Your clean credit report is your vision board for financial freedom. Make it plain, make it accurate, make it powerful.

Your credit report is about to become your testimony of restoration. Every error removed is a chain broken. Every correction is a truth established. This is kingdom work—bringing order to chaos, truth to deception, and freedom to bondage.

***

Breaking Down the Bureaus vs. Services: Know Who Really Controls Your Data

The Big 3 Credit BUREAUS (The Actual Power Players):

- **Equifax, Experian, and TransUnion**—these are the actual credit bureaus (also called Credit Reporting Agencies or CRAs)
- They're billion-dollar corporations that collect, store, and sell your credit data
- They have legal authority under the Fair Credit Reporting Act to

maintain your credit files
- They're who lenders report to and pull reports from

Credit SERVICES/Monitoring Companies (The Middlemen):

- Credit Karma, Credit Sesame, MyFICO, IdentityForce, etc.
- These are businesses that buy your data from the bureaus and repackage it
- They make money through ads, affiliate links, and premium subscriptions
- They can't change your credit report—only help you see it

"But test everything; hold fast what is good" (1 Thessalonians 5:21). The bureaus hold your actual data; the services just show you what the bureaus already have. When disputing errors, you go straight to the source—the bureaus themselves, not the monitoring services. Understanding this distinction saves time, money, and frustration in your credit repair journey.

***

Section 1: Spotting Errors & Wielding Legal Weapons - Your Credit Report Combat Manual

The Hidden Thieves: Spotting Errors That Steal Your Future

"Be sober-minded; be watchful. Your adversary the devil prowls around like a roaring lion, seeking someone to devour" (1 Peter 5:8).

Credit errors are financial demons hiding in plain sight. The Federal Trade Commission found that 1 in 4 consumers have errors serious enough to affect their credit scores. These aren't innocent mistakes—they're profit centers for bureaus who get paid whether the information is accurate or not.

The Seven Deadly Credit Sins to Hunt For:

1. **Zombie Debts** - Accounts that should be dead but keep resurrection
    - Debts past the 7-year reporting limit
    - Re-aged accounts (illegal reset of the clock)
    - Sold debts appearing as new accounts
2. **Identity Theft Footprints**
    - Unknown addresses (thieves' drop locations)
    - Inquiries from companies you've never contacted
    - Accounts opened when you were a child or deployed
3. **Payment History Lies**
    - On-time payments marked late
    - Settled accounts showing as unpaid
    - Current accounts showing in collections
4. **Balance Inflation**
    - Credit limits reported lower than actual (kills utilization)
    - Balances showing higher than ever owed
    - Paid-off accounts showing balances

"You shall not bear false witness against your neighbor" (Exodus 20:16). When bureaus report lies about you, they're bearing false witness for profit.

Freezing Your Credit: The Ultimate Shield

The Four Guardians You Must Command:

1. **Equifax:** equifax.com/personal/credit-report-services | 1-800-349-9960
2. **Experian:** experian.com/freeze | 1-888-397-3742
3. **TransUnion:** transunion.com/credit-freeze | 1-888-909-8872
4. **Innovis** (the hidden 4th bureau): innovis.com/personal/securityFreeze | 1-800-540-2505

Don't forget **ChexSystems** (for bank accounts): consumerdebit.com | 1-800-428-9623

"Above all else, guard your heart, for everything you do flows from it" (Proverbs 4:23). Guard your credit like your heart—freeze it until YOU decide to open it.

The Legal Nuclear Option: FCRA Section 1681s-2(b)

Here's the weapon credit repair companies charge $3,000 to use—now it's yours for free:

15 U.S.C. § 1681s-2(b) - "Duties of Furnishers Upon Notice of Dispute"

This law states that when you dispute through the credit bureau, the original creditor (furnisher) MUST:

- Conduct a reasonable investigation
- Review all relevant information you provide
- Report results to ALL credit bureaus
- Correct or delete inaccurate information
- Not report information they know is inaccurate

The Power Move: When you cite this specific code, you're putting the creditor on legal notice. Violations can cost them $1,000 per incident plus your actual damages and attorney fees.

The Collection Killer Strategy: The 2-Year Doctrine

While collections can legally report for 7 years, here's what the pros know:

Why Target 2+ Year Old Collections:

- Debt buyers often can't validate old debts (no original documents)
- Original creditors have destroyed records
- Statutes of limitations may have expired for lawsuits
- Older debts have less impact—removing them boosts scores more

The Method of Execution: "Under **15 U.S.C. § 1681g**, I demand validation of this alleged debt. As this account is over 2 years old and you have failed to provide contemporaneous documentation proving the validity, accuracy, and ownership of this debt, it must be removed immediately under **§ 1681i(a)(5)(A)**."

The Affidavit Arsenal: Sworn Statements That Force Action

"But let your 'Yes' be 'Yes,' and your 'No,' 'No.' For whatever is more than these is from the evil one" (Matthew 5:37).

Affidavits are sworn testimony that carry legal weight. Here's your template arsenal:

Identity Theft Affidavit: "I, [Name], swear under penalty of perjury that:

1. The account [#] was opened fraudulently without my knowledge or consent
2. I did not receive any goods, services, or money from this account
3. I have filed a police report [#] regarding this identity theft
4. I request immediate removal under **FCRA § 1681c-2**"

Error Correction Affidavit: "I, [Name], swear under penalty of perjury that:

1. I have never been 30+ days late on account [#]
2. Attached are bank statements proving all payments were made on time
3. This error has damaged my credit score by approximately [X] points
4. I demand correction within 30 days under **FCRA § 1681i**"

Your 30-Day Legal Battle Plan

Week 1: Intelligence Gathering

- Pull all reports, document every error
- File police reports for identity theft
- Freeze all credit files
- Gather all supporting documents

Week 2: Launch Legal Strikes

- Send certified letters citing specific **FCRA** sections
- Include affidavits with notary seals
- Demand investigation under **§ 1681i**
- Threaten liability under **§ 1681s-2(b)**

Week 3: Document Everything

- Keep all certified mail receipts
- Log every phone call
- Screenshot online disputes
- Build your legal file

Week 4: Escalate and Execute

- File CFPB complaints for non-responses
- Contact attorneys for willful non-compliance
- Prepare small claims court documents
- Calculate your

***

Section 2: The CFPB Complaint - Your Federal Enforcement Squad

When Credit Bureaus Ignore You: Calling in the Cavalry

"If your brother or sister sins, go and point out their fault, just between the two of you. If they listen to you, you have won them over. But if they will not listen, take one or two others along... If they still refuse to listen, tell it to the church" (Matthew 18:15-17).

You've sent certified letters. You've waited 30 days. The credit bureaus are playing dead, hoping you'll give up. This is when you escalate to their oversight authority—the Consumer Financial Protection Bureau (CFPB). Think of it as taking your case before the federal judges who can actually force action.

Understanding the CFPB's Divine Authority

The CFPB isn't just another toothless agency. Created after the 2008 financial crisis, they have:

- Power to fine companies millions for violations
- Authority to order immediate corrections
- Public database that shames non-compliant companies
- Direct pipeline to company executives who MUST respond

"Let everyone be subject to the governing authorities, for there is no authority except that which God has established" (Romans 13:1). The CFPB is an authority God has allowed for your protection—use it.

The 15-Day Miracle: How CFPB Complaints Force Action

When you file a CFPB complaint, companies have exactly **15 days** to respond or face regulatory scrutiny. Here's what happens behind the scenes:

1. Your complaint triggers an executive escalation
2. Compliance officers (not customer service) must handle it
3. Response becomes public record
4. Pattern of complaints triggers investigations
5. Non-response can result in consent orders and fines

Real Results: In 2023, the CFPB handled over 1.3 million complaints, returning $2.7 billion to consumers. Your complaint isn't just a form—it's a federal case.

Your Step-by-Step CFPB Battle Plan

Step 1: Gather Your Arsenal

- All correspondence with credit bureaus
- Certified mail receipts showing 30+ days passed
- Your original dispute letters
- Any responses (or proof of non-response)

Step 2: File Your Complaint at ConsumerFinance.gov/Complaint

Select Category: "Credit Reporting" → "Incorrect information on report"

Write Your Narrative (Template): "I disputed inaccurate information on my credit report with [Bureau Name] on [Date] via certified mail #[Tracking]. Federal law requires investigation within **30 days**. It has been [X] days with no response. The disputed information includes [specific accounts/errors]. This **violation of FCRA § 1681i** damages my credit score and financial opportunities. I request immediate investigation and correction."

Step 3: Attach Evidence

- Upload dispute letters
- Include certified mail receipts
- Add any bureau responses
- Document your damages

Step 4: Track and Escalate

- CFPB assigns a case number immediately
- Company must respond in 15 days
- If unsatisfactory, you can dispute their response
- CFPB mediates until resolution

The Nuclear Option: When to Name Names

"Therefore, having put away falsehood, let each one of you speak the truth with his neighbor" (Ephesians 4:25).

In your CFPB complaint, be specific:

- Name the exact employee who refused to help
- Quote any dismissive responses verbatim
- Detail how many times you've attempted resolution
- Calculate your actual damages (denied credit, higher rates)

Sample CFPB Complaint That Gets Results

"On [Date], I discovered TransUnion reporting a Capital One collection account #XXX that was paid in full in 2019. I disputed this error on [Date] with certified documentation proving payment. TransUnion's 30-day deadline expired on [Date].

They have:

- Failed to investigate as required by **FCRA § 1681i**
- Continued reporting false information violating § 1681e(b)
- Caused my score to remain artificially low by 75+ points
- Cost me $3,000 in higher interest on my car loan

I've attached all documentation. I request TransUnion immediately delete this paid account and provide written confirmation. Their willful non-compliance has caused measurable financial harm."

The Multiplication Effect

When you file a CFPB complaint:

- It goes into a public database
- Regulators see patterns of violations
- Class action attorneys monitor for cases
- Media researchers track company violations
- Your single complaint joins thousands demanding justice

"Two are better than one, because they have a good return for their labor" (Ecclesiastes 4:9). Your complaint alone is powerful; combined with others, it's unstoppable.

Your Rights After Filing

If They Don't Respond in 15 Days:

- CFPB marks them as non-responsive (public record)
- You can escalate to CFPB management
- Opens door for legal action with documented federal violation

If They Respond But Don't Fix:

- Dispute their response through CFPB portal
- Provide additional documentation
- Request CFPB mediation
- Consider "willful non-compliance" legal action

The Kingdom Perspective on Righteous Advocacy

"Learn to do right; seek justice. Defend the oppressed" (Isaiah 1:17).

Filing a CFPB complaint isn't complaining—it's commanding companies to honor truth. You're not just fixing your credit; you're holding billion-dollar corporations accountable for bearing false witness. Every complaint filed is a stone thrown at Goliath.

Remember: David didn't defeat Goliath with his own strength—he used the tools available and trusted God for victory. The CFPB is your sling, your complaint is your stone, and federal law is your battlefield. Now go claim your victory.

Your Next Action: If it's been 45 days since your CFPB complaint and the credit bureau still refuses to correct or delete the errors, you've entered "willful non-compliance" territory. This is where righteous warriors separate from those who merely complain.

The Legal Acceleration Path

Document Your Damages:

- Every credit denial letter (with dates)

- Higher interest rates you've paid (calculate the difference)
- Lost job opportunities (many employers check credit)
- Emotional distress documentation (anxiety, sleepless nights)
- Time spent fighting errors (your time has value)

Small Claims Court Strategy:

- File for $1,000-$5,000 (varies by state)
- No lawyer needed
- Credit bureaus rarely show up (automatic win)
- Federal law violations = easy verdict
- Use template: "Defendant violated **FCRA § 1681i** by failing to investigate and correct known errors after 30-day statutory deadline"

The Attorney Letter Advantage: Many consumer attorneys work on contingency for FCRA violations. One letter from a law firm often produces instant deletion. Search "FCRA attorney [your city]" for free consultations.

"Do not be overcome by evil, but overcome evil with good" (Romans 12:21). Your persistence in pursuing truth overcomes their evil of bearing false witness.

When All Else Fails: The Public Testimony

- Post your CFPB case number on social media tagging the bureau
- Share in credit repair forums with documentation
- Contact local news consumer reporters
- File Better Business Bureau complaints
- Write executive office emails (CEO/President)

The Multiplication Principle: Your public testimony warns others and creates pressure. Credit bureaus fear viral stories more than individual complaints.

Remember: Every David needs persistence to defeat Goliath. Your sling is loaded, your aim is true, and the law is on your side. Keep throwing stones until the giant falls. Your breakthrough is someone else's blueprint—fight not just for your victory, but for theirs.

***

Section 3: How to Win Damages Against Collection Agencies - Turning Violations Into Victory

Building Your Federal Case: From Victim to Victor

"But let justice roll down like waters, and righteousness like an ever-flowing stream" (Amos 5:24).

Every illegal collection call, every false threat, every harassing letter isn't just an annoyance—it's a $1,000 paycheck waiting to be collected. The Fair Debt Collection Practices Act doesn't just protect you; it pays you. Most people endure abuse from collectors, not knowing that each violation can be converted into cash damages, deleted debts, and legal victories.

Today you learn how to build an airtight case that makes collection agencies write YOU checks.

The Affidavit of Truth: Your Sworn Sword

"Above all, my brothers and sisters, do not swear—not by heaven or by earth or by anything else. All you need to say is a simple 'Yes' or 'No.' Otherwise you will be condemned" (James 5:12).

A notarized Affidavit of Truth carries the weight of sworn testimony. It transforms your word into legal evidence that can't be easily dismissed. Here's your template:

AFFIDAVIT OF TRUTH

State of [Your State] County of [Your County]

I, [Your Name], being first duly sworn, do hereby state under penalty of perjury:

1. On [Date] at [Time], I received a call from [Collector Name] of [Agency Name] at phone number [Their Number].
2. The collector violated 15 USC 1692 as follows:
    - Threatened arrest/criminal prosecution (§1692e(4))
    - Called before 8am/after 9pm (§1692c(a)(1))
    - Used profane/abusive language (§1692d(2))
    - Called repeatedly to harass (§1692d(5))
    - Contacted me after cease-and-desist (§1692c(c))

3. I have documented evidence attached as Exhibit A-[X].
4. These violations caused me [specific damages: lost sleep, anxiety, lost wages, etc.].
5. I swear the above statements are true and correct.

[Your Signature]
Subscribed and sworn before me this ___ day of ________, 20__
Notary Public

Marking the Collection Letter: Creating Exhibit Evidence

When you receive collection letters, don't throw them away—they're evidence worth thousands. Here's your marking system:

Step 1: Make 3 Copies

- Original stays untouched in plastic sleeve
- Copy 1: For marking violations
- Copy 2: For your records
- Copy 3: For your attorney

Step 2: Mark Every Violation Using a RED pen, circle and annotate:

- False amount claimed → "§1692e - False representation"
- Threats of lawsuit beyond SOL → "§1692e(5) - Threat of illegal action"
- "Refusal to pay" language → "§1692e(10) - False representation"
- Missing disclosures → "§1692g - Validation notice violation"

Step 3: Create Your Evidence Log Date: [Date received] Violation #1: [Specific quote] = §[Code section] = $1,000 Violation #2: [Specific quote] = §[Code section] = $1,000 Total Violations This Letter: $[Amount]

"A false witness will not go unpunished, and whoever pours out lies will not go free" (Proverbs 19:5). Every marked violation is exposing their false witness.

The Invoice Strategy: Billing Your Abusers

Here's where you flip the script completely—you send THEM a bill:

INVOICE FOR FDCPA VIOLATIONS

Invoice #: [Your initials]-[Date]-001 Date: [Current Date]
Bill To: [Collection Agency Name] [Their Address]
Re: FDCPA Violation Damages - Account #[XXX]
LINE ITEMS:

- Violation of §1692c(c) - Contact after cease-and-desist: $1,000
- Violation of §1692d - Harassment/abuse (3 instances): $3,000
- Violation of §1692e - False representations (2 instances): $2,000
- Actual damages - Lost wages documenting violations: $500
- Emotional distress requiring counseling: $1,500

TOTAL DUE: $8,000

Payment Terms: Net 30 days After 30 days, legal action will commence for collection.

This invoice represents statutory and actual damages under 15 USC 1692k. Payment constitutes settlement of all claims.

The Certified Mail Power Play

"Let what you say be simply 'Yes' or 'No'; anything more than this comes from evil" (Matthew 5:37).

Certified mail with return receipt is your "Yes" that can't be denied:

Your Certified Mail Checklist:

- [ ] USPS Certified Mail (not FedEx/UPS)
- [ ] Return Receipt Requested (green card)
- [ ] Tracking number documented
- [ ] Copy of envelope showing addresses
- [ ] Photo of sealed envelope with contents visible
- [ ] Keep all receipts forever

The Strategic Sequence:

1. Send invoice with affidavit via certified mail
2. Wait 30 days (document any contact - more violations)
3. If unpaid, send "Final Notice Before Legal Action"
4. File in small claims court (no attorney needed)

5. Serve them (they rarely show up)

Your Damage Documentation Arsenal
Build your case file:

- **Call Log**: Date, time, number, name, violations
- **Recording**: (If legal in your state) Save all files
- **Letters**: Original plus marked copies
- **Emails**: Print everything
- **Witnesses**: Anyone who heard calls
- **Damages**: Therapy bills, lost wages, medical costs

The Court Victory Formula
Small claims court loves FDCPA cases:

- Filing fee: $50-$200 (recoverable)
- No attorney needed
- Judges know FDCPA well
- Collectors rarely appear (default judgment)
- Typical awards: $1,000-$5,000 plus fees

Your Court Presentation: "Your Honor, I have documented [X] violations of federal law. Here is my notarized affidavit, marked evidence, certified mail receipts, and invoice showing attempts to resolve. I request statutory damages of $1,000 per violation plus my actual damages of $[X]."

Remember: *"Do not be overcome by evil, but overcome evil with good" (Romans 12:21).* You're not being vindictive—you're holding lawbreakers accountable. Every dollar you collect in damages is a dollar they can't use to abuse another consumer. Your victory becomes someone else's protection.

Start documenting. Start invoicing. Start collecting. The hunters are about to become the hunted.

Chapter 3: The Truth About Collections & Charge-Offs

Demystifying the Debt Graveyard

"Then you will know the truth, and the truth will set you free" (John 8:32).

Collections and charge-offs are the financial world's scarlet letters—marks of shame designed to follow you for seven years. But here's what they don't want you to know: These aren't death sentences, they're negotiation opportunities. Every collection account has a price tag, every charge-off has an expiration date, and every debt collector has a breaking point.

What Really Happens When Accounts Go Bad

The Charge-Off Lie When a creditor "charges off" your debt after 120-180 days, they're writing it off for tax purposes—but you still owe it. They've already claimed the tax deduction, then they sell your debt for pennies on the dollar. The debt buyer paid maybe $50 for your $5,000 debt, yet they'll harass you for the full amount plus interest.

"Dishonest scales are an abomination to the Lord, but a just weight is His delight" (Proverbs 11:1). Demanding $5,000 for a $50 investment is the definition of dishonest scales.

The Collection Food Chain

1. Original creditor charges off (gets tax write-off)
2. Sells to debt buyer #1 for 3-5 cents per dollar
3. Debt buyer #1 fails, sells to buyer #2 for 1-2 cents
4. Debt buyer #2 fails, sells to buyer #3 for fractions of pennies
5. Each sale makes documentation weaker and validation harder

The Seven-Year Myth and the Zombie Debt Truth

Collections can legally report for 7 years from the date of first delinquency—not from when it was sold, not from last payment, not from when they feel like it. But here's what happens:

Illegal Re-Aging Tactics:

- Updating the "date opened" when debt is sold
- Reporting old debt as new to reset the clock
- Creating "duplicate" accounts to double the damage
- Claiming any payment restarts the 7-year clock (FALSE)

"You shall not steal, nor deal falsely, nor lie to one another" (Leviticus 19:11). Re-aging debt is stealing years of your financial life.

Your Rights: The Weapons They Hope You Don't Know

Right #1: Debt Validation (Your "Prove It" Power) Within 30 days of first contact, you can demand they prove:

- You owe the debt
- They own the debt
- The amount is correct
- They have legal right to collect

Most can't prove all four. No proof = must delete.

Right #2: Cease and Desist (Your "Shut Up" Power) One letter can legally stop all calls, letters, and contact. They can only sue you after that—and most won't for debts under $1,000.

Right #3: Statute of Limitations (Your "Too Late" Power) Each state has deadlines for lawsuit filing:

- Credit cards: Usually 3-6 years
- Medical debt: Usually 4-6 years
- Written contracts: Usually 4-10 years

After the deadline, debt becomes "zombie debt"—legally uncollectable but still reportable.

The Settlement Secret Formula

Here's the math collectors don't want you to understand:

- They paid: 1-5% of original balance
- They'll profit at: 10-15% of original balance
- They'll celebrate at: 25% of original balance

- They're lying when they say: "We can't go below 70%"

Real Example: $5,000 original debt

- Debt buyer paid: $50-$250
- Profitable settlement: $500-$750
- Your offer: Start at $250 (5%), settle at $500-$750 (10-15%)

"Suppose one of you wants to build a tower. Won't you first sit down and estimate the cost?" (Luke 14:28). Know their cost before negotiating.

The Pay-for-Delete Strategy

The holy grail of collections handling:

1. Negotiate settlement amount
2. Get agreement IN WRITING for deletion upon payment
3. Pay with cashier's check or money order
4. Keep proof forever
5. Dispute if not deleted within 30 days

Warning: Many collectors lie about pay-for-delete. If it's not in writing, it didn't happen.

The Charge-Off Chess Game

Charge-offs hit your credit twice—once as late payments leading up, once as the charge-off. But here's the strategic approach:

For Fresh Charge-Offs (Under 2 years):

- Negotiate directly with original creditor
- They still have authority to recall from collections
- Offer 40-60% for deletion or "paid as agreed" notation

For Old Charge-Offs (Over 2 years):

- Often sold multiple times
- Documentation is weak or lost
- Dispute first, negotiate second
- Many can't validate and must delete

Your Collections Battle Plan
Month 1: Validation Letters

- Send to every collector within 30 days
- Demand full documentation
- Do NOT admit owing anything

Month 2: Evaluate Responses

- No validation = dispute with bureaus
- Weak validation = negotiate hard
- Strong validation = settlement strategy

Month 3: Execute Strategy

- Pay-for-delete for newer debts
- Dispute older/unvalidated debts
- Let zombie debts die naturally

The Kingdom Perspective on Debt Resolution

"The wicked borrow and do not repay, but the righteous give generously" (Psalm 37:21).

This isn't about avoiding legitimate debts—it's about preventing predatory collectors from stealing more than they're owed. Pay what's truly owed, but don't let debt buyers profit from deception.

Remember: Jesus turned over the money changers' tables because they were thieves disguised as legitimate business. Many debt collectors operate the same way. Know your rights, stand your ground, and use wisdom to break free from both legitimate debt and illegitimate harassment.

Your charge-offs and collections are not your identity. They're temporary marks that time and strategy can erase. The same God who forgave your spiritual debt can guide you through forgiving financial ones—strategically, wisely, and completely.

***

Section 1: How to Challenge Invalid Debts - Your Validation Victory Guide

The Divine Right to Demand Proof

"Test everything; hold fast what is good" (1 Thessalonians 5:21).

God commands us to test everything—especially claims against our finances. When a debt collector calls claiming you owe money, they're making an accusation. Under federal law and Kingdom principles, every accuser must prove their case. The burden of proof is on THEM, not you.

Too many believers accept collectors' claims as gospel truth. They pay debts they don't owe out of fear, shame, or misplaced integrity. But paying an invalid debt isn't integrity—it's enabling deception. Today, you learn to wield the sword of validation.

Understanding Debt Validation: Your Legal Shield

The Fair Debt Collection Practices Act (FDCPA) gives you a powerful weapon: the right to validation. Within 30 days of first contact, you can demand collectors prove:

1. **The debt exists** (original contract with your signature)
2. **The amount is accurate** (full accounting of principal, interest, fees)
3. **They own the debt** (complete chain of title from original creditor)
4. **They're licensed** (to collect in your state)
5. **It's within statute** (not too old to legally collect)

"By the mouth of two or three witnesses every word shall be established" (2 Corinthians 13:1). If they can't provide witnesses (documentation), the debt isn't established.

The 30-Day Window: Your Critical First Move

The Clock Starts When:

- You receive their first written notice
- OR they first contact you by phone
- Whichever comes first triggers your 30-day right

What Happens If You Don't Validate:

- They assume the debt is valid
- They can continue collection efforts
- You lose your strongest leverage
- Courts may assume you accept the debt

"The prudent see danger and take refuge, but the simple keep going and pay the penalty" (Proverbs 27:12). Don't be simple—validate immediately.

Your Validation Letter Template

Send this via certified mail within 30 days:

[Your Name] [Your Address] [Date]

[Collector's Name] [Collector's Address]

Re: Account #[XXXXX] - Validation of Alleged Debt

Dear [Collector Name]:

I received your [letter/call] dated [date] regarding the above-referenced account. Under my rights pursuant to 15 USC 1692g, I formally request validation of this alleged debt.

Please provide the following:

1. Original signed contract creating the alleged debt
2. Complete payment history from original creditor
3. Documentation proving you own/have right to collect this debt
4. Proof of your license to collect debts in [your state]
5. Accounting showing how the current amount was calculated

Under FDCPA § 1692g(b), all collection activity must cease until validation is provided. I am disputing this debt and exercising all rights under federal law.

This is not an acknowledgment of any debt. All future communications must be in writing.

Sincerely, [Your Signature] [Your Typed Name]

What Valid Validation Actually Looks Like

They MUST Provide:

- Original creditor's records (not their summary)
- Your actual signature on original agreement
- Complete chain of ownership if debt was sold
- Itemized accounting of every charge
- Proof amount hasn't exceeded legal interest limits

What Doesn't Count:

- Computer printouts with your name
- Their own affidavits saying you owe
- Collection letters from previous collectors
- Partial records or summaries
- "Screen shots" of their computer system

"Dishonest scales are an abomination to the Lord, but a just weight is His delight" (Proverbs 11:1). Incomplete validation is a dishonest scale.

When They Can't or Won't Validate

If They Don't Respond in 30 Days:

- They must cease all collection efforts
- They cannot report to credit bureaus
- Any continued collection violates FDCPA
- You can sue for $1,000 per violation

If Their Validation Is Weak:

- Point out specific deficiencies in writing
- Demand complete validation or deletion
- File complaints with CFPB and state attorney general
- Dispute with credit bureaus citing failed validation

Common Collector Tricks:

- "We'll validate after you pay something" (ILLEGAL)
- "Validation request time has expired" (FALSE - can request anytime)

- "We don't need to validate" (VIOLATES federal law)
- "Your payment history is validation" (INSUFFICIENT)

The Nuclear Option: Validation During Lawsuit

If they sue without proper validation:

1. Answer the lawsuit (don't ignore!)
2. Include "Failure to validate debt" as a defense
3. Demand validation in discovery
4. File counterclaim for FDCPA violations
5. Most dismiss rather than prove invalid debt

"If anyone wants to sue you and take your shirt, hand over your coat as well" (Matthew 5:40). But first, make them prove you owe the shirt!

Your Strategic Validation Timeline

Day 1-5: Validation letter sent certified mail **Day 6-35**: Document all contact attempts (violations) **Day 36**: If no response, send "failure to validate" letter **Day 40**: Dispute with all credit bureaus **Day 45**: File CFPB complaint **Day 60**: Consider legal action for violations

Red Flags of Invalid Debts

Watch for these signs the debt is bogus:

- Amount differs from what you remember owing
- Debt is older than your state's statute of limitations
- Collector can't name original creditor
- They threaten arrest or criminal charges
- Amount keeps changing
- They refuse to send anything in writing

"My people are destroyed for lack of knowledge" (Hosea 4:6). Know these signs and protect yourself.

The Kingdom Perspective on Invalid Debts

"You shall not bear false witness against your neighbor" (Exodus 20:16).

When collectors claim debts they can't prove, they're bearing false witness. You're not avoiding legitimate obligations—you're demanding truth in financial matters. Every invalid debt you challenge protects not just your finances but prevents that collector from victimizing others.

Remember: Jesus confronted religious leaders who "devoured widows' houses" through false religious obligations. Modern debt collectors often do the same through false financial obligations. Stand firm, demand proof, and don't pay Caesar what Caesar can't prove you owe.

Your validation letter isn't just paperwork—it's a declaration that truth matters, proof is required, and your financial future won't be hijacked by unproven claims. Send it, track it, and watch invalid debts crumble under the weight of truth.

***

Section 2: Cease-and-Desist Letters, Debt Validation & Settlement Strategies - Your Triple Threat Playbook

Cease-and-Desist: Your Right to Peace

"Come to me, all you who are weary and burdened, and I will give you rest" (Matthew 11:28).

When debt collectors call 20 times a day, harass your family, or threaten you at work, they're not just violating federal law—they're stealing your peace. God promises rest, but collectors profit from your torment. The cease-and-desist letter is your legal right to silence their harassment while you plan your strategy.

What Cease-and-Desist Actually Does:

- Legally stops ALL communication (calls, letters, texts)
- Forces them to either sue or leave you alone
- Protects your workplace from embarrassing calls
- Gives you breathing room to think clearly
- Creates evidence if they violate the order

Your Cease-and-Desist Template:

[Send Certified Mail]

RE: Cease and Desist All Communication - Account #[XXX]

Under my rights pursuant to 15 USC 1692c(c), I hereby demand you cease all communication with me regarding the above-referenced account.

Do not contact me by:

- Phone (home, work, or cell)
- Mail (except legal service)
- Email or text message
- Third parties (family, employer, neighbors)

You may only communicate through proper legal channels if you choose to pursue judicial remedies. Any violation will result in legal action for damages under FDCPA.

This is not an acknowledgment of any debt.

[Your Signature] [Date]

"In peace I will lie down and sleep, for you alone, Lord, make me dwell in safety" (Psalm 4:8). You have the right to peaceful sleep without collector calls.

Debt Validation: Making Them Prove It

While cease-and-desist stops communication, validation challenges the debt's very existence. Use them strategically:

The One-Two Punch Strategy:

1. Send validation request FIRST (within 30 days)
2. Wait for their response (or non-response)
3. If validation is weak/missing, send cease-and-desist
4. They're now trapped: can't collect, can't communicate

Advanced Validation Tactics:

The "Chain of Title" Demand: "Provide complete chain of title from original creditor to current collector, including:

- All purchase agreements
- Bills of sale with my account specifically listed
- Assignment documentation
- Proof each company was licensed in my state"

Most debt buyers can't produce this. No chain = no right to collect.

The "Original Contract" Test: "Provide the original contract I allegedly signed, not:

- Terms and conditions from website
- Generic cardholder agreements
- Unsigned applications
- Recreated documents"

"Where there is no guidance, a people falls, but in an abundance of counselors there is safety" (Proverbs 11:14). Demand every document—their lack of documentation is your counsel for victory.

Settlement Strategies: The Art of the Deal

Once you've validated (or they've failed to), it's time to negotiate. Remember: they bought your $5,000 debt for $50-$250. Everything above their cost is profit.

The Settlement Hierarchy:

Best Outcome: Pay-for-Delete

- Complete removal from credit report
- Get agreement in writing FIRST
- Pay with cashier's check
- Keep proof forever
- Worth paying 40-50% for deletion

Good Outcome: Paid-as-Agreed

- Shows as paid in full, never late
- Rebuilds credit faster than "settled"
- Negotiate for 30-40% of balance

Acceptable Outcome: Settled-for-Less

- Still negative but shows resolved
- Pay 20-30% maximum
- Better than outstanding collection

The 609 Settlement Script: "I'm prepared to resolve this matter today for [25% of balance]. In exchange, you'll:

1. Mark the account 'Paid as Agreed' on all credit reports
2. Provide written confirmation before payment
3. Accept this as payment in full
4. Never sell or reassign this debt

This offer expires in 7 days. After that, I'll proceed with validation disputes."

Timing Your Triple Threat

Month 1: Information Gathering

- Pull credit reports
- List all collections/charge-offs
- Note dates, amounts, collectors

Month 2: Validation Assault

- Send validation letters to all collectors
- Document everything
- Prepare for non-responses

Month 3: Strategic Decisions

- Cease-and-desist non-validators
- Negotiate with those who validated
- Dispute with bureaus for non-responders

Month 4-6: Settlement Season

- Use tax refunds or bonuses
- Negotiate hardest at month-end (quotas)
- Get everything in writing

The Psychology of Collector Negotiations

"Be wise as serpents and innocent as doves" (Matthew 10:16).

What Collectors Fear Most:

- Bankruptcy (they get nothing)
- Statute of limitations expiring
- FDCPA lawsuits
- Bad publicity/complaints
- Month-end without meeting quotas

Use Their Fear As Leverage:

- "I'm meeting with a bankruptcy attorney next week..."
- "My FDCPA attorney says I have a strong case..."
- "The statute of limitations expires in 6 months..."
- "I'm prepared to pay today, but only for deletion..."

Your Settlement Commandments

1. **Never Pay Without Written Agreement** *"Let what you say be simply 'Yes' or 'No'" (Matthew 5:37).* If it's not in writing, it's not real.
2. **Never Give Bank Account Access**
    - Use cashier's checks or money orders only
    - Never authorize automatic withdrawals
    - Protect your accounts from "accidental" over-drafting
3. **Never Admit Owing the Debt**
    - Say: "I'm willing to pay $X to resolve this matter"
    - Not: "I know I owe this and want to pay"
    - Admissions can restart statute of limitations
4. **Always Keep Perfect Records**
    - Record calls (if legal in your state)
    - Save all letters and emails
    - Document dates, times, names
    - Create a "victory file" for each debt

The Kingdom Perspective on Strategic Settlement

"Agree with your adversary quickly, while you are on the way with him" (Matthew 5:25).

Jesus taught strategic settlement—not because you're guilty, but because sometimes peace is worth more than being right. Every dollar saved through negotiation is a dollar available for Kingdom purposes. Every hour not spent fighting collectors is an hour available for your calling.

Remember: You're not cheating anyone by negotiating. The original creditor already wrote off the debt and took tax benefits. The debt buyer is a speculator who bought risk. Your offer of 25% gives them 500% profit on their investment. That's more than fair—that's generous.

Your cease-and-desist letter brings peace. Your validation demand brings truth. Your settlement offer brings resolution. Together, they bring freedom. Use all three weapons wisely, and watch your financial bondage transform into financial breakthrough.

***

Section 3: What Happens When You Pay vs. When You Negotiate - The Credit Report Truth

The Hidden Cost of "Just Paying"

"The simple believe anything, but the prudent give thought to their steps" (Proverbs 14:15).

When you receive a collection notice demanding $3,000 and simply pay it, you might feel virtuous—but you've just made three costly mistakes. First, you've validated a debt that might have been invalid. Second, you've paid 10-20 times what the collector paid for it. Third, and most devastating: you've locked in negative credit reporting for seven more years.

Here's the brutal truth: **Paying a collection doesn't improve your credit score.** It changes the status from "unpaid collection" to "paid collection"—both are negative marks that hurt your score almost equally. You've spent thousands for almost no credit benefit.

The Credit Report Reality Check

When You Just Pay in Full:

- Status updates to: "Paid Collection" (still negative)
- Remains on report: Full 7 years from original delinquency
- Score improvement: 0-10 points (negligible)
- Future lenders see: You had a collection (red flag)
- Your leverage: Gone forever

When You Negotiate Properly:

- Status can be: Deleted entirely (pay-for-delete)
- Or: "Paid as Agreed" (positive notation)
- Or: "Settled for Less" (less negative than collection)
- Score improvement: 50-150 points (for deletion)
- Future lenders see: Clean history or resolved account
- Your leverage: Maximized before payment

"Plans fail for lack of counsel, but with many advisers they succeed" (Proverbs 15:22). Paying without negotiating is planning without counsel.

The Mathematics of Strategic Settlement

Let's expose the real numbers:

Collection for $3,000 - Just Paying:

- You pay: $3,000
- Collector paid: $90 (3% of original)
- Their profit: 3,233%
- Your credit benefit: Minimal
- Time on report: 7 years

Same Collection - Smart Negotiation:

- You pay: $750 (25% settlement)
- Collector still profits: 733%
- Your savings: $2,250
- Your credit benefit: Potential deletion
- Time on report: 0 years (if deleted)

The Power Dynamic Shift

When you just pay, you're communicating:

- "I accept your terms"
- "I don't know my rights"
- "I'm desperate"
- "I'll pay whatever you demand"

When you negotiate, you're declaring:

- "I know this debt cost you pennies"
- "I understand my legal rights"
- "I have options, including bankruptcy"
- "Let's find a win-win solution"

"The rich rule over the poor, and the borrower is slave to the lender" (Proverbs 22:7). But through negotiation, you break the slave mentality and deal as equals.

Your Negotiation Leverage Points

Before You Pay, You Have:

1. **The Validation Threat** - They might not be able to prove the debt
2. **The Bankruptcy Card** - They get nothing in bankruptcy
3. **The Statute of Limitations** - Time might run out for lawsuits
4. **The Complaint Option** - CFPB, attorney general, bad reviews
5. **The Cash Incentive** - Immediate payment vs. long collection process

After You Pay, You Have: Nothing. Zero. Nada.

The Settlement Conversation Script

Wrong Way (Just Paying): "Hi, I got your letter. Where do I send the $3,000?"

Right Way (Strategic Negotiation): "I'm calling to resolve account #XXX. I've been advised to file bankruptcy, but I'd prefer to settle this today. I can offer $600 as payment in full if you can email me an agreement for pay-for-delete within the hour. This offer expires when I hang up, as I have three other collectors to call. What email should I watch for your agreement?"

The Biblical Balance of Negotiation

"If it is possible, as far as it depends on you, live at peace with everyone" (Romans 12:18).

Negotiation isn't about cheating anyone—it's about finding peaceful resolution that honors the true economics of the situation. The original creditor already took tax deductions. The debt buyer is a speculator who bought risk. Your negotiated settlement gives them profit while preserving your financial future.

Kingdom Math:

- Money saved through negotiation = more for tithes and offerings
- Credit score preserved = ability to be a blessing to others

- Stress reduced = more energy for ministry
- Wisdom gained = testimony to share

Your Pre-Payment Checklist
Before paying ANYTHING:

- [ ] Validation letter sent and response received
- [ ] Settlement agreement in writing
- [ ] Exact credit reporting language specified
- [ ] Payment method that protects your accounts
- [ ] Copies made of all documents
- [ ] Recording of agreement (if legal)
- [ ] Prayer for wisdom completed

Remember: Once you pay, your leverage evaporates like morning dew. But when you negotiate first, you're using the same wisdom Solomon used when he said, *"The buyer says, 'It's no good, it's no good!' but then goes off and boasts about the purchase"* (Proverbs 20:14).

Don't be the seller who accepts the first offer. Be the wise negotiator who knows the true value and settles strategically. Your future self—and your credit score—will thank you.

***

Section 4: Sample Letters, Validation Tactics & Pushback Strategies - Your Battle-Tested Arsenal

When Collectors Push Back: Standing Your Ground

"Be strong and courageous. Do not be afraid or terrified because of them, for the Lord your God goes with you; He will never leave you nor forsake you" (Deuteronomy 31:6).

When you assert your rights, collectors often push back with intimidation, lies, and manipulation. They're counting on your fear and ignorance. But armed with the right letters and responses, you become David facing down Goliath—except this time, you've got an entire arsenal of stones.

The Master Validation Letter That Terrifies Collectors

This letter combines every legal requirement and strategic demand:

[SEND CERTIFIED MAIL WITH RETURN RECEIPT]

[Your Name] [Your Address] [Date]

[Collection Agency Name] [Their Address]

RE: Validation of Alleged Debt - Account #[XXX] CERTIFIED MAIL #[Tracking Number]

Dear Debt Collector:

I received your [letter/call] dated [date] regarding the above-referenced account. Under my rights pursuant to the Fair Debt Collection Practices Act, 15 USC 1692g, I formally dispute this alleged debt and demand validation.

YOU MUST PROVIDE:

1. Original contract bearing my signature
2. Proof of your ownership/assignment of this specific debt
3. Complete chain of title from original creditor
4. Full accounting showing:
    - Original balance
    - All payments credited
    - All interest/fees with dates and legal basis
    - How current amount was calculated

5. Proof debt is within statute of limitations for [State]
6. Your license to collect debts in [State]
7. Surety bond information per state requirements

LEGAL NOTICE:

- Under FDCPA § 1692g(b), all collection activity must cease until validation is provided
- Any continued collection attempts will be considered harassment under § 1692d
- Reporting unvalidated debt violates FCRA § 1681s-2(b)
- I am recording all calls and documenting all violations
- Time-barred debt collection attempts may violate state law

This letter serves as notice that I am aware of my rights and will exercise them fully. Any information obtained will be used for the purpose of determining the validity of this alleged debt.

This is not an acknowledgment of any debt, nor a promise to pay. I reserve all rights.

Sincerely, [Your Signature] [Your Typed Name]

cc: Consumer Financial Protection Bureau cc: [State] Attorney General cc: Better Business Bureau

When They Push Back: Your Counter-Strike Responses

Pushback #1: "Validation period has expired"

Your Response: "The 30-day period is for disputing, not requesting validation. I can request validation at any time under continuous rights doctrine. Please provide validation or cease collection attempts."

"The one who states his case first seems right, until the other comes and examines him" (Proverbs 18:17). Don't let them state false law unchallenged.

Pushback #2: "We already sent validation"

Your Response: "A computer printout is not validation. Please provide the specific documents outlined in my letter: original contract, chain of title, and complete accounting. Your failure to provide proper validation is noted."

Pushback #3: "Pay something to show good faith"

Your Response: "Any payment before validation would waive my rights and reset the statute of limitations. I will not make any payment until you prove this debt is valid, owned by you, and legally collectible. This appears to be an attempt to trick me into waiving federal protections."

The Cease-and-Desist Nuclear Option

When they won't validate but keep harassing:

CEASE AND DESIST ALL COMMUNICATION

[Certified Mail Details]

RE: Cease and Desist Order - Failed Validation

You have failed to provide proper validation as requested on [date]. Under 15 USC 1692c(c), I demand you:

CEASE ALL COMMUNICATION immediately regarding this unvalidated debt. You may not:

- Call me at any number
- Contact my employer
- Contact my family/references
- Send letters except legal service
- Report to credit bureaus
- Transfer/sell this unvalidated debt

Your only option is proper legal action, where you'll need to prove validation in court.

VIOLATIONS DOCUMENTED:

- [List dates/times of illegal contact]
- [List false statements made]
- [List threats or harassment]

I am prepared to file suit for FDCPA violations. Each violation = $1,000 statutory damages plus actual damages and attorney fees.

[Your Signature]

Advanced Validation Tactics

The "Forensic Accounting" Demand: "Provide a complete forensic accounting showing every transaction, fee, interest calculation, and payment from account opening to present. Include the legal basis for each charge and mathematical proof the amount is correct."

The "Original Creditor Trap": "Since you claim to own this debt, provide written confirmation from [Original Creditor] that they sold this specific account to you and have no further interest in it."

The "License Check": "Provide proof of your license/registration to collect debts in [State]. Include bond information and any complaints filed against your license."

"The simple believe anything, but the prudent give thought to their steps" (Proverbs 14:15). These tactics separate legitimate collectors from scavengers.

Your Pushback Response Scripts

When They Threaten Lawsuit: "I welcome the opportunity to have a judge review your lack of validation. Please ensure your attorney brings all original documents I've requested. I'll be countersuing for FDCPA violations."

When They Claim "Refusal to Pay": "I'm not refusing to pay valid debts. I'm exercising my federal right to validation. Your characterization of legal rights as 'refusal' is noted as a potential FDCPA violation."

When They Get Aggressive: "This call is being recorded. Your aggressive tone and false statements violate FDCPA § 1692d. Continue, and I'll add this to my federal complaint."

The Documentation Victory Plan

1. **Create a War Chest**
    - Folder for each debt
    - Copy of every letter sent
    - Certified mail receipts
    - Call log with dates/times/names
    - Recording of calls (if legal)
2. **Build Your Evidence**
    - Screenshot all credit report entries
    - Save all voicemails
    - Print all emails
    - Note all witnesses to calls

3. **Track Their Violations**
    - Each call after cease-and-desist = $1,000
    - Each false statement = $1,000
    - Each credit report after dispute = $1,000
    - Threatening arrest = $1,000
    - Calling your work after told not to = $1,000

Remember: *"If God is for us, who can be against us?" (Romans 8:31).* When you stand on truth and law, even billion-dollar collection agencies must yield. Your validation letters aren't just paper—they're swords of truth cutting through deception. Your pushback responses aren't just words—they're shields protecting your peace and prosperity.

Keep fighting. Keep documenting. Keep believing. Your breakthrough is built one letter, one response, one victory at a time.

Part II: Rebuild & Reposition - From Survivor to Strategist

Your Resurrection Season Begins Now

"Therefore, if anyone is in Christ, the new creation has come: The old has gone, the new is here!" (2 Corinthians 5:17).

Decoding the system was your diagnosis. Now comes your cure. Part II isn't about credit repair—it's about complete financial resurrection. You're not going back to where you were. You're positioning yourself where the wealthy operate: above the system, not under it.

This section transforms you from credit victim to credit victor. You'll discover that rebuilding isn't about begging for approval—it's about strategic positioning. The same tools that enslaved you will now elevate you. The same system that rejected you will now compete for your business.

In Part II, you'll master:

- Credit builder loans that pay YOU to improve your score
- The tradeline secret that can add 100 points in 30 days
- How to turn secured cards into unsecured credit lines
- Score optimization tricks that cost nothing but knowledge
- Why the wealthy have 20+ credit cards (and how to do it safely)
- The exact timeline from bankruptcy to 800 credit score
- How to position yourself for business credit (your second credit file)

"He lifted me out of the pit of despair, out of the mud and the mire. He set my feet on solid ground and gave me a firm place to stand" (Psalm 40:2). Your credit resurrection isn't just about numbers—it's about identity. You're learning to think like a lender, not a borrower. To see opportunity where others see obstacles. To build wealth where others just seek approval.

By the end of Part II, you won't just have better credit—you'll have a completely different relationship with money. You'll be the one making the system work for you, not the other way around. Your rebuilding becomes your testimony. Your repositioning becomes your platform for generational wealth.

Remember: The same God who resurrected Christ can resurrect your credit. But first, you must believe it's possible. Then, you must learn the strategies. Finally, you must execute with discipline.

Your breakthrough starts with knowledge and manifests through action. Let's begin.

Chapter 4: Credit Builder Loans & Secured Accounts - Your Credit Resurrection Tools

The Wisdom of Starting Small

"Whoever is faithful in very little is also faithful in much, and whoever is dishonest in very little is also dishonest in much" (Luke 16:10).

Credit builder loans and secured accounts are God's training ground for financial faithfulness. While the world mocks you for starting over with "baby steps," Heaven celebrates every act of discipline. These aren't tools for the desperate—they're strategic weapons for the wise who understand that empires are built one brick at a time.

The wealthy use these same tools to build credit for their children, establish business credit profiles, and test new banking relationships. You're not behind—you're beginning where wisdom dictates: with secured foundations.

Credit Builder Loans: The Backwards Blessing

Here's the divine reversal that confuses the world but delights Heaven: With credit builder loans, you make payments BEFORE receiving money. It's like tithing—giving first, receiving after. The bank holds your "loan" amount in a savings account while you make monthly payments. Only after you've proven faithful do you receive the funds.

How It Works:

1. You "borrow" $1,000 (bank holds it in savings)
2. You pay $85/month for 12 months
3. Bank reports perfect payments to all bureaus
4. You receive your $1,000 plus interest at the end
5. Your credit score increases 35-100 points

Best Credit Builder Loan Providers:

- **Self** (formerly Self Lender): $25-$150/month plans, reports to all 3 bureaus
- **Credit Strong**: Offers up to $1,000 monthly payments for

aggressive building

- **Digital Federal Credit Union**: No fees, competitive rates
- **Navy Federal**: Military families, excellent terms

"The plans of the diligent lead to profit as surely as haste leads to poverty" (Proverbs 21:5). This is diligence manifested—paying for credit you'll receive later.

Secured Credit Cards: Your Covenant Collateral

Like Abraham offering Isaac, secured cards require you to put up what's precious (your cash) to receive what's promised (credit history). Your deposit becomes your credit limit, but the rewards far exceed the sacrifice.

The Strategic Approach:

1. **Start with 2-3 secured cards** (different banks)
2. **Deposit more than minimum** ($500-$1,000 if possible)
3. **Use only 1-3%** of limit ($5-$30 on a $1,000 card)
4. **Automate one small bill** per card
5. **Pay in full before statement date**

Top Secured Card Champions:

- **Discover it® Secured**: Cashback rewards, graduates to unsecured
- **Capital One Platinum Secured**: Low deposit options
- **OpenSky® Secured**: No credit check required
- **Chime Credit Builder**: No deposit, builds from checking

The Hidden Power of Secured Accounts

"A good name is more desirable than great riches; to be esteemed is better than silver or gold" (Proverbs 22:1).

Your payment history on secured accounts weighs the SAME as millionaire's payments. The credit algorithm doesn't discriminate between secured and unsecured—it only sees faithfulness. This is your opportunity to build a "good name" in the financial realm.

The Multiplication Strategy:

- Month 1-6: Perfect payments on all secured accounts
- Month 7: Request credit limit increases (without adding deposit)
- Month 9: Apply for first unsecured card
- Month 12: Graduate secured cards to unsecured
- Month 18: 700+ credit score achieved

Your Secured Account Battle Plan
Week 1: Foundation

- Open high-yield savings for credit builder loan parking
- Research and choose 2-3 secured cards
- Set aside deposit funds

Week 2: Activation

- Apply for credit builder loan
- Apply for secured cards (space by 1 week)
- Set up automatic payments

Week 3: Optimization

- Add one small recurring bill to each card
- Set up autopay for full balance
- Create payment tracking spreadsheet

Month 2-12: Execution

- Never miss a payment (automate everything)
- Keep utilization under 3%
- Don't close accounts
- Monitor credit weekly

The Graduation Timeline
Months 1-6: Foundation Building

- Credit score increase: 35-50 points

- Status: "Credit Rookie"

Months 7-12: Momentum Phase

- Credit score increase: 50-75 more points
- Status: "Credit Climber"
- Milestone: First unsecured approval

Months 13-18: Acceleration

- Total increase: 100-150 points
- Status: "Credit Graduate"
- Achievement: 700+ score possible

"Though your beginning was small, yet your latter end would increase abundantly" (Job 8:7). Your secured accounts are the "small beginning" that prophesies abundant increase.

Avoiding the Secured Account Traps

Trap #1: High Annual Fees Some cards charge $99+ yearly. Calculate if rewards offset fees.

Trap #2: Non-Reporting Cards Verify they report to ALL THREE bureaus before applying.

Trap #3: Non-Graduating Cards Choose cards that convert to unsecured and return deposits.

Trap #4: Overspending Temptation Just because you have $1,000 limit doesn't mean use it.

The Kingdom Perspective

Remember: You're not rebuilding credit because you worship FICO scores. You're rebuilding because *"The borrower is slave to the lender" (Proverbs 22:7)*, and good credit makes you the lender's desired partner, not their slave. Every on-time payment preaches a sermon about faithfulness. Every graduated card testifies to transformation.

Your secured accounts are seeds. Plant them wisely, water them with discipline, and watch them grow into a forest of financial opportunities.

The same God who multiplied loaves and fishes can multiply your faithful payments into supernatural credit restoration.

Start small. Stay faithful. Graduate gloriously.

***

Section 1: Best Banks and Credit Unions for Your Credit Resurrection

Choosing Your Financial Allies Wisely

"Plans fail for lack of counsel, but with many advisers they succeed" (Proverbs 15:22).

Not all financial institutions are created equal when it comes to rebuilding credit. Some banks see you as a risk to avoid; others see you as a future success story worth investing in. The difference between rejection and approval often isn't your credit score—it's choosing the right partner for your resurrection journey.

The Credit Union Advantage: Where Members Matter

Credit unions operate like financial churches—they exist to serve members, not maximize profits. This fundamental difference makes them powerful allies for credit rebuilding.

Navy Federal Credit Union (The Military's Best-Kept Secret)

- Open to military, veterans, and their families
- **nRewards Secured Card**: Graduates in as little as 6 months
- **Credit Builder Loan**: Up to $3,000 with flexible terms
- **Fresh Start Checking**: No ChexSystems denial
- Known for manual underwriting (they look beyond scores)

"Bear one another's burdens, and so fulfill the law of Christ" (Galatians 6:2). Navy Federal literally bears their members' financial burdens during rebuilding.

PenFed Credit Union (The Hidden Gem)

- Anyone can join with a small donation
- **Secured Platinum Card**: Low $250 minimum deposit
- **Personal Loans**: Starting at $600 for credit building
- Reports to all three bureaus religiously
- Graduates secured cards faster than most

Local Credit Unions (Your Neighborhood Allies)

- Search: NCUA.gov credit union locator
- Benefits: Personal relationships, flexible underwriting
- Often offer "fresh start" programs
- Second chance checking when banks say no

The Big Bank Rebuilders: When Goliath Helps David
Chase Bank (The Surprising Second-Chance Giant)

- **Chase Credit Journey**: Free credit monitoring for everyone
- **Slate Edge℠** : Easier approval than traditional Chase cards
- **Secure Banking℠** : Second chance checking account
- Strategy: Start with checking, build relationship, then apply for credit

Capital One (The Rebuilder's Friend)

- **Platinum Secured**: Minimum $49 deposit
- **QuicksilverOne**: For fair credit (not subprime)
- Pre-qualification without hard inquiry
- Known for credit limit increases with good behavior

Discover (The Graduation Champion)

- **Discover it® Secured**: Only major secured card with rewards
- Automatic graduation reviews starting month 7
- Matches all cashback first year (doubling rewards)
- Free FICO score monthly

"Whoever is kind to the poor lends to the Lord, and he will reward them for what they have done" (Proverbs 19:17). These banks profit by helping you rebuild—a divine business model.

The Online Bank Revolution

Chime (The Disruptor)

- **Credit Builder Card**: No deposit, builds from checking
- **SpotMe**: Overdraft protection without fees
- Early direct deposit (get paid 2 days early)
- No credit check to open

Self (The Credit Builder Specialist)

- Combines savings with credit building
- Choose your monthly payment ($25-$150)
- CD-secured installment loans
- Partners with Lead Bank for legitimacy

Varo (The All-in-One)

- **Varo Believe**: Secured card with no annual fee
- Automatic credit line increases
- High-yield savings to park your deposits
- No foreign transaction fees

Your Strategic Banking Timeline
Month 1-3: Foundation Phase

1. Open checking at a credit union AND one big bank
2. Set up direct deposit (shows stability)
3. Apply for secured cards at different institutions
4. Start smallest credit builder loan

Month 4-6: Relationship Building

- Use checking accounts actively
- Pay any fees immediately
- Save consistently (they monitor this)
- Request pre-qualifications

Month 7-12: Expansion Phase

- Apply for unsecured products where you bank
- Request credit limit increases
- Add authorized user status if available
- Graduate secured products

The Multi-Bank Strategy
"In abundance of counselors there is victory" (Proverbs 11:14).
Don't put all your eggs in one basket:

- **Credit Union**: For personal touch and flexibility
- **Major Bank**: For credit cards and business services
- **Online Bank**: For high-yield savings and innovation
- **Community Bank**: For future mortgage relationships

Red Flags to Avoid
Predatory "Second Chance" Banks:

- Excessive monthly fees ($20+)
- Required expensive add-ons
- Don't report to credit bureaus
- No path to regular accounts

Signs of Good Rebuilding Partners:

- Clear graduation paths
- Free credit education
- Multiple product options
- Reasonable fees
- Actual humans you can talk to

Your Application Strategy

1. **Start Where You Have History**: Existing relationships matter
2. **Apply on Tuesdays**: Best approval rates (less volume)
3. **Call Reconsideration Lines**: Human review beats algorithms
4. **Document Your Story**: Explain past issues, show current stability

5. **Leverage Direct Deposit**: Steady income covers many credit sins

Remember: *"Ask and it will be given to you; seek and you will find; knock and the door will be opened to you" (Matthew 7:7).* Sometimes the best banks for rebuilding are the ones willing to hear your story, not just see your score. Build relationships, not just accounts. Your next banker might be the angel assigned to your financial breakthrough.

***

Section 2: How to Use Secured Cards and Installment Loans Strategically - The Chess Master's Guide

Playing the Long Game with Secured Cards

"The wise store up choice food and olive oil, but fools gulp theirs down" (Proverbs 21:20).

Getting a secured card isn't the strategy—it's what you do with it that separates credit builders from credit champions. Most people treat secured cards like training wheels, using them heavily until they can get "real" credit. This is backwards. The wealthy use multiple credit lines like a chess master uses pieces—each one positioned strategically, most barely moving, all serving the greater game.

The 1-3-5 Rule for Secured Cards:

- 1% utilization on your primary secured card (one small subscription)
- 3% maximum on any single card ever
- 5% total utilization across all cards combined

Here's the strategic setup: Get three secured cards from different banks, put $500-$1,000 on each. Now you have $1,500-$3,000 in available credit. Use only $15-$30 TOTAL across all three. This shows the algorithm you have massive self-control and multiple banking relationships.

The Installment Loan Power Move

"Let no debt remain outstanding, except the continuing debt to love one another" (Romans 13:8).

While secured cards prove you can manage revolving credit, installment loans prove you can handle fixed obligations. But here's the strategy most miss: You don't need the money. You need the payment history.

The Credit Builder Loan Ladder:

1. Start with a $300 loan for 12 months ($25/month)
2. At month 4, add a $600 loan for 12 months ($50/month)

3. At month 8, add a $1,000 loan for 12 months ($85/month)

Now you have THREE positive payment streams reporting monthly. By month 12, you've got 36 positive payment records (3 loans × 12 months) plus your original loan completing successfully. Your credit mix is diversified, your payment history is bulletproof, and you've saved the money anyway.

The Strategic Timeline That Changes Everything

Months 1-3: Foundation

- Open secured card #1 with $1,000 deposit
- Put Netflix on it ($15/month)
- Start $300 credit builder loan
- Focus: Perfect payments, low utilization

Months 4-6: Expansion

- Add secured card #2 with $500 deposit
- Put Spotify on it ($10/month)
- Add $600 credit builder loan
- Total utilization: Still under 3%

Months 7-9: Acceleration

- Add secured card #3 with $500 deposit
- Put cloud storage on it ($2/month)
- Consider $1,000 credit builder loan
- Request credit limit increases without adding deposits

Months 10-12: Graduation

- Apply for unsecured cards with same banks
- Graduate secured cards to unsecured
- Complete first credit builder loan
- Credit score increase: 100-150 points typical

The Hidden Strategies That 10X Your Results

Strategy #1: The Statement Date Hack Pay your secured cards to zero 5 days BEFORE the statement date. The bureaus see 0% utilization, but the bank sees activity. You get perfect scoring without looking inactive.

Strategy #2: The Multiple Bank Advantage Each bank reports slightly differently. Chase might report on the 1st, Capital One on the 15th, Discover on the 30th. This creates constant positive activity in your credit file—the algorithm loves fresh positive data.

Strategy #3: The Authorized User Amplifier While building your own credit, get added as an authorized user on someone's established card. Don't even get the physical card. Their history becomes your history. Combined with your strategic building, you're attacking from both sides.

"Two are better than one, because they have a good return for their labor" (Ecclesiastes 4:9). Your secured accounts plus authorized user status equals exponential growth.

The Mathematics of Strategic Building

Let's expose what really happens:

- 3 secured cards × 12 months = 36 payment records
- 3 installment loans × varied terms = 36-48 more records
- Total positive records in one year: 72-84
- Each record worth 1-2 points: 72-168 point potential

Compare this to one secured card used normally: 12 records, maybe 20-30 points gained.

Your Strategic Commandments

1. **Never Max Out Secured Cards** - Even though it's your money, utilization is utilization
2. **Automate Everything** - Manual payments introduce risk; automation ensures perfection
3. **Document Your Strategy** - Screenshot scores monthly to track what works
4. **Stay the Course** - Month 6 feels slow; month 12 brings the harvest
5. **Reinvest Your Returns** - When loans mature, use funds for next level building

Remember: *"Whoever can be trusted with very little can also be trusted with much" (Luke 16:10).* These secured tools are your "very little"—master them strategically, and watch Heaven trust you with much. Every automated payment preaches faithfulness. Every low utilization demonstrates wisdom. Every completed loan prophesies your financial future.

You're not just building credit—you're building character, one strategic decision at a time.

***

Section 3: Apple Federal Credit Union - The 5% Interest Credit Builder Secret

The Hidden Gem of Credit Building

"Go to the ant, you sluggard; consider its ways and be wise! It has no commander, no overseer or ruler, yet it stores its provisions in summer and gathers its food at harvest" (Proverbs 6:6-8).

While everyone chases big banks with flashy ads, Apple Federal Credit Union quietly offers one of the most powerful credit-building combinations available: secured credit cards backed by savings accounts earning up to 5% APY. You're literally getting PAID to rebuild your credit—a divine reversal where your discipline generates dividends.

The Apple FCU Advantage Decoded

Apple Federal Credit Union (serving anyone who lives, works, or worships in Northern Virginia, DC area, or joins through partner organizations) has created what I call the "Double Harvest Strategy":

Their Secured Visa® Card:

- Minimum deposit: Just $250
- Your deposit earns dividends while securing your card
- Reports to all three credit bureaus
- No annual fee
- Graduates to unsecured with good payment history

Their High-Yield Savings:

- Up to 5.00% APY on balances up to $1,000
- 0.50% APY on balances over $1,000
- No monthly fees
- Perfect parking spot for your secured card deposit

"Whoever gathers money little by little makes it grow" (Proverbs 13:11). Your secured deposit isn't sitting idle—it's growing at 5% while building your credit simultaneously.

The Strategic Mathematics That Changes Everything

Let's expose the genius of this system:

Traditional Secured Card:

- $1,000 deposit sits earning 0%
- You pay $50-99 annual fee
- Net cost: $50-99 per year

Apple FCU Strategy:

- $1,000 deposit earns 5% = $50/year
- No annual fee = $0 cost
- Net PROFIT: $50 per year
- Plus: Credit score increases 50-100 points

You're literally being PAID $50 annually to rebuild your credit!

Your Apple FCU Implementation Blueprint

Step 1: Membership Qualification

- Live/work/worship in eligible areas, OR
- Join American Consumer Council ($8 lifetime)
- Open basic savings with $5

Step 2: The High-Yield Foundation

- Open Money Market Savings
- Deposit $1,000 for maximum 5% rate
- Set up automatic transfer to maintain balance

Step 3: Secured Card Activation

- Apply for Secured Visa
- Use your high-yield savings as collateral
- Set one small recurring bill
- Automate full payment

Step 4: The Growth Cycle

- Month 1-6: Perfect payments, minimal usage
- Month 7: Request credit limit increase
- Month 12: Apply for graduation to unsecured
- Ongoing: Keep earning 5% on your money

Advanced Apple FCU Strategies

The Ladder Method: Start with $250 secured card, then every 3 months:

- Add another $250 to deposit
- Request limit increase
- Build to $1,000 (maximum 5% interest)
- Multiple increases show financial growth

The Family Builder:

- Open accounts for spouse/children
- Each gets 5% on their $1,000
- Family of 4 = $200/year interest income
- Everyone builds credit simultaneously

"Train up a child in the way he should go; even when he is old he will not depart from it" (Proverbs 22:6). Teaching credit building while earning interest—double wisdom.

The Complete Apple FCU Arsenal

Beyond secured cards, leverage their full suite:

- **Credit Builder Loans**: Competitive rates
- **Share Certificates**: Higher yields for longer commitments
- **Free Financial Counseling**: Personal credit coaching
- **Skip-a-Pay Options**: Grace during tough months

Your 90-Day Apple FCU Action Plan

Days 1-30:

- Join through qualifying method
- Open high-yield savings with $1,000
- Let account season while earning 5%

Days 31-60:

- Apply for secured card
- Set up one subscription
- Automate payments
- Monitor credit weekly

Days 61-90:

- Verify bureau reporting
- Calculate interest earned
- Plan next deposit increase
- Share testimony with others

Remember: *"The blessing of the Lord brings wealth, without painful toil for it" (Proverbs 10:22).* Apple FCU has created a system where your money works while you sleep, building credit and earning interest simultaneously. This isn't just smart—it's supernatural multiplication in action.

Your secured deposit becomes a seed that grows two harvests: restored credit and compound interest. Plant wisely, tend faithfully, and reap abundantly.

I searched for information about Apple Federal Credit Union, but the results showed Apple Card's savings account instead. Let me search more specifically for Apple FCU's credit builder products.

Keshia, based on current data, Apple FCU offers some solid options but not quite the 5% you mentioned. Here's what they actually offer:

Apple FCU's Best Current Rates:

- **EdVantage Savings**: 3.00% APY on balances up to $10,000 (for educators)
- **Coverdell ESA**: 5.00% APY (but restricted to education expenses)

- **Student Savings (eXtras)**: 3.00% APY up to $1,499
- **Credit Builder Card**: Secured deposit earns regular savings rate (0.10% currently)

The Strategic Alternative: While Apple FCU's Credit Builder secured card is excellent (no annual fee, graduates to unsecured), pair it with their **EdVantage account** if you qualify as an educator for 3% on your emergency fund.

For true 5% rates right now, consider:

- **Mango Savings**: Up to 5% on $2,500
- **Digital Federal Credit Union**: Often competitive rates
- **T-Mobile Money**: 4% on first $3,000 with qualifying plan

The credit-building strategy remains powerful—using higher-yield savings to secure your credit builder card means your deposit works twice: building credit AND earning interest. Even at 3%, that's $30/year on a $1,000 deposit while your credit score climbs.

***

Section 4: Apple FCU's Complete Credit Building Arsenal: Beyond Cards to Strategic Loans

The Credit Builder Loan Revolution

"For which of you, desiring to build a tower, does not first sit down and count the cost, whether he has enough to complete it?" (Luke 14:28)

Apple Federal Credit Union doesn't just offer secured cards—they've created an entire ecosystem of credit-building loans designed to resurrect your financial reputation. Their loan programs work like training wheels that pay you to learn.

Apple FCU's Credit Builder Loan Program:

- **Amounts**: $500 to $3,000
- **Terms**: 12-24 months
- **How it works**: Funds held in savings while you make payments
- **Interest rates**: As low as 5.00% APR
- **Special feature**: Your payments earn dividends while building credit

The Share-Secured Loan Strategy

This is Apple FCU's best-kept secret for aggressive credit building:

How Share-Secured Loans Work:

1. You deposit $1,000 in savings (earning dividends)
2. Borrow against your own money at low rates (2-3% above dividend rate)
3. Make monthly payments that report to all bureaus
4. Keep your savings intact and growing
5. Build installment loan history without risk

The Genius Math:

- Savings earning: 0.10% (regular) or up to 3% (special accounts)

- Loan rate: Typically 3% above your dividend rate
- Net cost: Only 3% on money you're not using
- Credit benefit: Adds crucial installment history

"The rich rule over the poor, and the borrower is slave to the lender" (Proverbs 22:7). But when you borrow against your own money, you're both lender and borrower—breaking the slavery cycle.

The Auto Loan Credit Accelerator

Apple FCU's vehicle loans offer unexpected credit-building power:

First-Time Buyer Program:

- Designed for limited credit history
- Lower down payment requirements
- Rates starting at 5.74% APR
- Builds major installment history
- Can refinance to lower rate after 12 months

Strategic Auto Loan Approach:

1. Buy used car under $10,000
2. Put 20% down ($2,000)
3. Finance $8,000 for 36 months
4. Payments around $235/month
5. Refinance after year one at better rate

The Student Loan Advantage

Apple FCU Student Loans:

- No payments while in school
- 0.25% rate discount for auto-pay
- Can consolidate existing student loans
- Parents can transfer to student later
- Builds long-term credit history

"Start children off on the way they should go, and even when they are old they will not turn from it" (Proverbs 22:6). Building credit during college sets lifetime patterns.

The Complete Apple FCU Credit Building Stack

Here's how to layer their products for maximum impact:

Year 1 Foundation:

- Month 1: Open savings, deposit $1,000
- Month 2: Get secured credit card
- Month 3: Add $500 credit builder loan
- Month 6: Add share-secured loan (**STOP**: Refer for Section 5: Before you continue.)

Year 2 Acceleration:

- Graduate secured card to unsecured
- Add auto loan if needed
- Increase credit builder loan to $1,000
- Request credit line increases

By Year 2 End:

- 4+ active trade lines
- 24+ months of perfect payments
- Mixed credit types (revolving + installment)
- 650-750 credit score typical

The Hidden Benefits of Apple FCU Membership

Financial Counseling:

- Free one-on-one credit coaching
- Debt management planning
- Budget creation assistance
- Credit report review

Skip-a-Pay Program:

- Skip one loan payment per year
- No negative credit impact
- Small fee ($35) vs. late payment damage
- Perfect for emergency situations

Relationship Pricing:

- Each product you have reduces rates on others
- Checking + savings + loan = better rates
- Loyalty rewards for long-term members

Your 12-Month Apple FCU Domination Plan
Months 1-3:

- Join and establish membership
- Open high-yield savings options
- Start with secured card + credit builder loan
- Automate everything

Months 4-6:

- Add share-secured loan
- Perfect payment history building
- Monitor credit weekly
- Build relationship with loan officers

Months 7-9:

- Request credit increases
- Consider auto loan if needed
- Add authorized user status
- Prepare for graduation

Months 10-12:

- Graduate to unsecured products

- Celebrate 50-100 point increase
- Plan next level strategies
- Share testimony

Remember: *"Well done, good and faithful servant! You have been faithful with a few things; I will put you in charge of many things" (Matthew 25:23).* Apple FCU's loan programs are your "few things"—master them faithfully, and watch Heaven open doors to greater financial authority.

Their system isn't just about building credit—it's about building character, discipline, and a testimony of transformation that no credit score can fully capture. However, do not start the initiation of these strategies if your financial health is unstable, not dependable, or your money is below what is required to follow through with the full process. We'll touch on income possibilities and side hustles that will turn these circumstances around with some planning and inside tips for starting a profitable business from nothing.

***

Section 5: The Financial Prerequisites for Apple FCU Credit Building Success

Your Ready-to-Build Financial Checklist

"For which of you, wanting to build a tower, doesn't first sit down and calculate the cost to see if he has enough to complete it?" (Luke 14:28)

Before launching this credit-building stack, you need honest assessment of your financial foundation. Whether you are seeking to implement this financial strategy with Apple FCU or any other financial institution, consider the reality of your actual financial condition or income at the present time. You are seeking to build your credit, not put it into question by not meeting the payments expectations or requirements on any of the loans you may qualify for. Seek to improve your financial discipline and intelligence about your own spending, income, and respect the rules of any and all financial institutions you are contracted with. Now, for the previous plan to work, this strategy requires approximately $2,000 in seed money and $150-200 monthly cash flow for loan payments.

Minimum Financial Health Requirements:

Income: $2,500+ monthly take-home pay

- Covers basic expenses with $500+ leftover
- Stable for at least 6 months
- Can be from multiple sources

Savings: $3,000 minimum recommended

- $1,000 for secured deposits
- $1,000 for share-secured loan
- $1,000 emergency buffer (don't touch)

Monthly Cash Flow: $200+ after all bills

- $45 for credit builder loan payment
- $85 for share-secured loan payment

- $70 buffer for life's surprises

Existing Obligations: Current on everything

- No recent late payments
- Basic bills manageable
- Not drowning in minimums

The Income Sweet Spots
$30,000-$40,000 Annual Income:

- Can execute basic strategy
- Focus on secured card + credit builder loan
- Add share-secured loan only if comfortable

$40,000-$60,000 Annual Income:

- Perfect for full strategy
- Room for all products plus buffer
- Can accelerate timeline

$60,000+ Annual Income:

- Can double deposits for faster results
- Add multiple products simultaneously
- Consider business credit building too

"Dishonest money dwindles away, but whoever gathers money little by little makes it grow" (Proverbs 13:11). This strategy is about consistent small payments, not large income.

Red Flags to Wait

Don't start if you have:

- Negative monthly cash flow
- No emergency fund
- Unstable employment

- Pending major expenses

Better to stabilize first than to start and fail. Your credit rebuilding testimony requires completion, not just good intentions.

***

Section 6: Honorable Mentions – Banks That Help You Build Credit with Integrity

The Power of Partnership in Financial Restoration

"Two are better than one, because they have a good return for their labor. If either of them falls down, one can help the other up" (Ecclesiastes 4:9–10).

When rebuilding credit, choosing the right financial institution is more than a transaction—it's a covenant. You're looking for banks and credit unions that don't just offer products, but walk with you through the process. These honorable mentions have earned reputations for supporting consumers with flexible tools, fair terms, and credit-building opportunities that align with biblical principles of stewardship, restoration, and wisdom.

Credit Unions That Champion the Underdog

KeyPoint Credit Union Based in California, KeyPoint offers secured credit cards and personal loans with competitive rates. Their community-first approach means they often look beyond your score to understand your story.

Digital Federal Credit Union (DCU) DCU is a national favorite for credit builder loans and secured cards. Their Credit Builder Loan allows you to save while building credit, and they report to all three bureaus. *"The plans of the diligent lead surely to abundance" (Proverbs 21:5).*

Nassau Federal Credit Union Serving New York communities, Nassau FCU offers second-chance checking and secured credit options. Their member services are known for compassion and flexibility.

Navy Federal Credit Union A top-tier institution for military families, Navy Federal's nRewards® Secured Card and Credit Builder Loan are among the best in the country. They graduate accounts quickly and offer generous credit limit increases.

Apple Federal Credit Union Apple FCU's secured card and credit builder loan programs are ideal for educators and community members. Their savings accounts also offer competitive interest, allowing your deposits to grow while your credit heals.

Alliance Credit Union Alliance offers secured cards and personal loans with low fees and a strong commitment to financial education. Their team often works one-on-one with members to create custom rebuilding plans.

Banks That Offer Strategic Credit Tools

PayPal PayPal's Credit and Pay Later programs report to bureaus and can help build revolving credit history. Their digital-first model is ideal for entrepreneurs and online earners.

Fifth Third Bank Known for its Momentum® Banking and secured card options, Fifth Third offers overdraft forgiveness and credit-building tools that reward consistency.

Regions Bank Regions provides secured credit cards and personal loans with flexible underwriting. Their "Now Banking" suite includes second-chance checking and budgeting tools.

Wells Fargo Wells Fargo's Secured Credit Card is one of the few that graduates to unsecured and offers rewards. Their credit education tools are robust and accessible.

PNC Bank PNC's Secured Visa® and credit builder loans are solid options for those rebuilding. They also offer virtual wallet tools to help manage spending and savings.

GM Financial (GM Bank) GM's credit-building auto loans are ideal for consumers needing a vehicle while rebuilding. They report monthly and offer refinancing options after 12 months of on-time payments.

BHG (Bankers Healthcare Group) BHG specializes in professional loans and credit-building tools for entrepreneurs and healthcare workers. Their underwriting is relationship-based, not just score-driven.

BMO Harris Bank BMO's Credit Builder Program includes secured cards and personal loans. Their customer service is known for transparency and support.

Fidelity Bank Fidelity offers secured cards and credit builder loans with competitive rates. Their financial literacy resources help consumers understand the "why" behind every product.

Building Credit with Honor and Wisdom

"The wise store up knowledge, but the mouth of a fool invites ruin" (Proverbs 10:14).

These institutions don't just offer products—they offer partnership. When you choose a bank that values your growth, you're aligning with Kingdom principles of restoration, stewardship, and legacy. Whether you're starting over or building for the first time, these honorable mentions can help you walk in financial victory.

Choose wisely. Steward faithfully. Build boldly. Your credit resurrection is not just possible—it's promised.

***

Section 7: Advanced Secured Card & Installment Loan Strategies - The Master Class

Beyond the Basics: When Good Strategy Becomes Great

"The simple inherit folly, but the prudent are crowned with knowledge" (Proverbs 14:18).

Dear reader, we covered the foundational secured card and installment loan strategies in the previous information, but let me give you the advanced playbook—the strategies that separate those who rebuild from those who dominate. These are the moves the credit repair companies charge thousands to reveal.

The **Velocity Method** for Secured Cards: Instead of one card with $1,000, get four cards with $250 each. Why? The credit algorithm values NUMBER of accounts with perfect payment history more than size of credit lines. Four cards = 48 positive payment records per year versus 12. Same money deployed, 4X the impact.

The Graduation Acceleration Hack: Most wait 12 months to graduate secured cards. But here's the secret: After 6 months of perfect payments, call and specifically ask for "product change to unsecured without hard inquiry." Many banks will do it early if you ask—they just don't advertise it. Now your deposit is freed for the next card while keeping the credit history.

The Installment Loan Ladder: Don't just get one credit builder loan. Stack them strategically:

Month 1: $300 loan for 12 months

Month 4: $500 loan for 18 months

Month 7: $1,000 loan for 24 months

This creates overlapping payment streams and shows increasing financial capacity. By month 12, you have three different installment accounts reporting perfect payments—credit mix maximized.

"In their hearts humans plan their course, but the Lord establishes their steps" (Proverbs 16:9). Plan your credit strategically, but let wisdom guide

your pace. These advanced strategies require discipline—only implement what you can faithfully maintain.

***

Section 8: The Power of Payment History and Utilization - Your 65% Credit Score Domination

Payment History: Your Financial Testimony Written Monthly

"Let your 'Yes' be 'Yes,' and your 'No,' 'No.' For whatever is more than these is from the evil one" (Matthew 5:37).

Payment history isn't just data—it's your character documented. Every month, you're writing your financial testimony across three credit bureaus. At 35% of your FICO score, payment history is the single most powerful factor in your credit resurrection. One late payment can drop your score 100 points. Twelve on-time payments can raise it 50+. The math is simple: Pay on time, every time, or pay the price for years.

Here's what the credit gods actually track:

- **On-time payments**: The only acceptable answer
- **30-day late**: Major damage, stays 7 years
- **60-day late**: Devastating, signals financial crisis
- **90-day late**: Often triggers charge-off
- **120-day late**: Account death, collection territory

The Kingdom Truth: Every payment is a promise kept. When you commit to a creditor, you're giving your word. Breaking it doesn't just hurt your score—it damages your testimony. *"It is better not to make a vow than to make one and not fulfill it" (Ecclesiastes 5:5).*

Utilization: The Discipline Score That Separates Winners from Wishers

"Like a city whose walls are broken through is a person who lacks self-control" (Proverbs 25:28).

Utilization—how much credit you use versus how much you have—accounts for 30% of your score. Together with payment history, these two factors control 65% of your financial destiny. But utilization is more psychological than mathematical. It measures restraint, not resources.

The Utilization Hierarchy:

- 0-9%: Elite status, maximum points
- 10-29%: Good, acceptable to lenders
- 30-49%: Warning zone, score drops
- 50-74%: Danger zone, major penalties
- 75%+: Financial emergency signal

The Secret: Utilization has no memory. Fix it today, see results in 30 days. This is grace in algorithm form—immediate forgiveness for immediate repentance.

The 65% Multiplication Strategy

Since payment history (35%) + utilization (30%) = 65% of your score, mastering these two creates exponential results:

Payment History Perfection Plan:

1. Automate every minimum payment
2. Set alerts 5 days before due dates
3. Pay manually in full after automation
4. Never close cards with perfect history
5. Let time multiply your testimony

Utilization Domination Method:

1. Calculate 1% of total available credit
2. Use only that amount monthly
3. Pay before statement dates
4. Request limit increases quarterly
5. Add new credit to lower percentage

"Whoever is faithful in very little is also faithful in much" (Luke 16:10). Master these two factors, and you've mastered most of the game.

The Hidden Power Moves

For Payment History:

- **Goodwill Letters**: Sometimes creditors remove single late payments

- **Re-aging**: Bringing current can reset the clock
- **Authorized User**: Inherit someone's perfect history

For Utilization:

- **Multiple Payment Method**: Pay twice monthly to show lower balances
- **Business Credit**: Doesn't count against personal utilization
- **Balance Alerts**: Set at 8% to never exceed 10%

Your 90-Day Transformation Formula
Days 1-30:

- Automate all payments
- Pay down to 9% utilization
- Document baseline score

Days 31-60:

- Request credit increases
- Add positive payment streams
- Watch score jump 25-50 points

Days 61-90:

- Optimize both factors
- Apply for strategic new credit
- Celebrate 50-100 point gain

Remember: These two factors are your credit foundation. Like faith and works, they operate together—payment history proves your faithfulness over time, utilization demonstrates your wisdom in the moment. Master both, and watch the other 35% of factors fall into place naturally.

"Therefore everyone who hears these words of mine and puts them into practice is like a wise man who built his house on the rock" (Matthew 7:24).

Payment history and utilization are your rock. Build everything else on this foundation.

***

Section 9: Advanced Secured Card & Installment Loan Strategies - The Master Class

Beyond the Basics: When Good Strategy Becomes Great

"The simple inherit folly, but the prudent are crowned with knowledge" (Proverbs 14:18).

Most people use secured cards like bicycles—basic transportation to get from bad credit to good. But the wealthy use them like private jets—sophisticated tools that take them exactly where they want to go, faster than anyone expects. The difference isn't the tool; it's the strategy.

The Velocity Method: Multiplication Over Addition

Traditional Thinking: Get one $1,000 secured card, use it responsibly, wait. **Advanced Strategy**: Deploy four $250 cards across different banks, creating a payment history machine.

Here's the divine math:

- 1 card × 12 months = 12 positive payments
- 4 cards × 12 months = 48 positive payments
- Same $1,000 invested, 4X the credit building power

Implementation:

1. Week 1: Capital One Secured ($250)
2. Week 3: Discover it Secured ($250)
3. Week 5: Credit One Secured ($250)
4. Week 7: Local credit union secured ($250)

"Give portions to seven, yes to eight, for you do not know what disaster may come upon the land" (Ecclesiastes 11:2). Diversification isn't just wisdom—it's biblical strategy.

The Graduation Acceleration Hack

The Secret Call Script: "Hi, I've been a perfect customer for 6 months. I'd like to discuss graduating my secured card to unsecured without a hard inquiry. Can you help me with a product change?"

Success Triggers:

- 6+ months perfect payments
- Account usage (small but consistent)
- No other negative marks
- Calling on Tuesday-Thursday (best approval rates)

If They Say No: "I understand. When would I be eligible? Can you note my account that I'm interested in graduation at the earliest opportunity?"

The Installment Loan Triple Stack

This strategy builds three different types of payment history simultaneously:

Stack Level 1 - The Foundation ($300/12 months):

- Provider: Self or local credit union
- Purpose: Establish installment history
- Payment: ~$25/month

Stack Level 2 - The Accelerator ($500/18 months):

- Provider: Different institution than Level 1
- Purpose: Show payment increase capability
- Payment: ~$30/month
- Start: Month 4

Stack Level 3 - The Maximizer ($1,000/24 months):

- Provider: Third institution
- Purpose: Demonstrate major loan management
- Payment: ~$45/month
- Start: Month 7

Total monthly commitment by month 7: ~$100 Total positive payment streams: 3 Credit mix optimization: Maximum

The Strategic Default Prevention System

"The wise see danger and take refuge, but the simple keep going and pay the penalty" (Proverbs 27:12).

Your Bulletproof Payment System:

1. **Primary**: Autopay from checking 5 days early
2. **Backup**: Calendar alerts 7 days before due
3. **Emergency**: Credit union overdraft protection
4. **Nuclear**: Skip-a-pay options documented

The 48-Hour Rule: If financial crisis hits, you have 48 hours to:

- Call every creditor
- Explain situation
- Request options
- Document everything

The Utilization Manipulation Method

Week 1 of Month:

- Use cards normally (staying under 10%)

Week 3 of Month:

- Pay all cards to $1-5 balance
- Let small balance report (shows activity)

Week 4 of Month:

- Pay remaining balance
- Score sees near-zero utilization

This creates the perfect algorithm impression: Active user with perfect control.

The Business Credit Bridge

While building personal credit, simultaneously build business credit:

1. Get EIN (free from IRS)
2. Open business checking
3. Get secured business card
4. Build second credit profile

"A good name is more desirable than great riches" (Proverbs 22:1). Now you're building TWO good names.

The Authorized User Amplifier

Advanced AU Strategy:

- Find someone with 10+ year perfect history
- Get added to their oldest card
- Don't get physical card
- Their history becomes yours
- Combine with your building for explosive growth

Your Month-by-Month Advanced Playbook

Months 1-3: Foundation

- Deploy 4 secured cards
- Start first installment loan
- Automate everything

Months 4-6: Acceleration

- Add second installment loan
- Request first limit increases
- Add authorized user status

Months 7-9: Multiplication

- Add third installment loan
- Begin graduation requests

- Monitor for 100+ point gains

Months 10-12: Domination

- Graduate secured cards
- Apply for premium cards
- Celebrate 700+ scores

***

Section 10: The Psychology & Spirit of Strategic Credit Building

Credit Building as Spiritual Warfare

"For our struggle is not against flesh and blood, but against the rulers, against the authorities, against the powers of this dark world" (Ephesians 6:12).

Strategic credit building isn't just financial—it's spiritual warfare. Every payment made on time is a declaration of faithfulness. Every temptation to overspend resisted is a victory over the flesh. Every strategic move that builds rather than destroys is alignment with Kingdom principles.

The Mindset Shifts That Change Everything

From Scarcity to Strategy:

- Scarcity: "I can barely afford minimums"
- Strategy: "I invest in credit building like a business"

From Shame to Authority:

- Shame: "I'm rebuilding because I failed"
- Authority: "I'm building because I'm destined to fund Kingdom work"

From Survival to Sovereignty:

- Survival: "I need credit for emergencies"
- Sovereignty: "I build credit to be a blessing"

The Discipline of Delayed Gratification

"Better is the end of a thing than its beginning, and the patient in spirit is better than the proud in spirit" (Ecclesiastes 7:8).

Strategic credit building requires:

- Paying for loans you don't receive immediately
- Keeping credit cards you don't use
- Maintaining accounts that cost money

- Waiting months to see results

This isn't natural—it's supernatural discipline. Each month of patience builds both credit and character.

The Testimony Hidden in Your Strategy

Your credit rebuilding journey is a sermon others need to hear:

- It proves God restores the broken
- It demonstrates wisdom over impulse
- It shows discipline conquers dysfunction
- It testifies that your past doesn't define your future

Remember: You're not just building credit—you're building a platform to fund churches, bless ministries, and leave generational wealth. Every strategic move today empowers Kingdom impact tomorrow.

***

Section 11: Foundations of Credit Resurrection – Secured Cards, Credit-Builder Loans, Rent Reporting, and Authorized User Strategies

Building Credit from the Ground Up

"Unless the Lord builds the house, the builders labor in vain" (Psalm 127:1).

Credit restoration begins with structure. Before you qualify for high-limit cards or business funding, you must lay a foundation of trust, consistency, and stewardship. Chapter 4 introduces the four pillars of credit resurrection—secured cards, credit-builder loans, rent reporting, and authorized user strategies. These tools are accessible, ethical, and powerful when used with wisdom. They don't just rebuild your score—they rebuild your testimony.

Secured Cards – The First Step Toward Trust

"Whoever can be trusted with very little can also be trusted with much" (Luke 16:10).

Secured credit cards are the training ground for financial discipline. You deposit your own money—typically $200 to $1,000—and the bank issues a credit card backed by that deposit. Every on-time payment is reported to the credit bureaus, proving your reliability.

Why It Works:

- Builds revolving credit history
- Reports monthly to all three bureaus
- Graduates to unsecured after 6–12 months
- Often comes with rewards and credit limit increases

Strategy:

- Use only 1–3% of your limit monthly
- Automate payments
- Request graduation after 6 months

This is your "yes" in the small things. It's not about the limit—it's about the legacy you're building through consistency.

Credit-Builder Loans – Installment History Without Risk

"The plans of the diligent lead surely to abundance" (Proverbs 21:5).

Credit-builder loans are installment loans where the bank holds the funds in a savings account while you make monthly payments. Once the loan is paid off, you receive the money—and a perfect payment history.

Benefits:

- Adds installment loan history
- Builds savings while building credit
- Reports monthly to all bureaus
- Can be stacked for greater impact

Strategy:

- Start with $300–$1,000 loan
- Choose 12–24 month term
- Automate payments
- Track progress monthly

This tool reflects biblical stewardship—paying faithfully, saving wisely, and reaping a harvest in due time.

Rent Reporting – Turning Your Home into a Credit Asset

"By wisdom a house is built, and through understanding it is established" (Proverbs 24:3).

Most people pay rent for years without realizing it can build credit. Rent reporting services allow you to report your monthly rent payments to the credit bureaus, adding positive history without taking on new debt.

Top Rent Reporting Services:

- RentReporters
- Esusu
- Piñata
- CreditMyRent

Why It Matters:

- Adds tradeline with 12–24 months of history
- Boosts score for thin files
- Reflects real-world responsibility

Strategy:

- Choose a service that reports to all three bureaus
- Backdate up to 24 months if possible
- Ensure landlord verification is smooth

Rent reporting turns your roof into a resource. It's proof that you've been faithful—even when no one was watching.

Authorized User Strategies – Borrowing Favor to Build Faith

"Two are better than one, because they have a good return for their labor" (Ecclesiastes 4:9).

Being added as an authorized user to someone else's seasoned credit card allows you to inherit their payment history, age, and limit. It's a legal and ethical way to boost your score—especially when your own credit is thin or damaged.

Best Practices:

- Choose cards with 5+ years of history
- Ensure utilization is under 10%
- Never request the physical card
- Remove yourself once your own credit is strong

Who to Ask:

- Parents
- Spouses
- Trusted friends
- Mentors

This is borrowed favor—like Ruth gleaning in Boaz's field. It's not permanent, but it's powerful when used with humility and gratitude.

Final Word: Build with Wisdom, Not Haste

These four tools—secured cards, credit-builder loans, rent reporting, and authorized user strategies—form the foundation of your credit resurrection. They are simple, accessible, and proven. But they require discipline, patience, and integrity.

"Do not despise these small beginnings, for the Lord rejoices to see the work begin" (Zechariah 4:10). Your credit journey may start small, but it's sacred. Every payment is a seed. Every report is a testimony. Every strategy is a step toward restoration.

Build wisely. Steward faithfully. And let your credit profile reflect the glory of a life rebuilt by grace and guided by truth.

Chapter 5: Tradelines - The Legal Hack to Accelerate Your Score

The Authorized User Anointing: Inheriting Credit Wisdom

"A good man leaves an inheritance to his children's children, but the wealth of the sinner is stored up for the righteous" (Proverbs 13:22).

Tradelines are the credit world's best-kept secret—a legal way to inherit someone else's perfect payment history. When you become an authorized user on an established account, their years of on-time payments become yours. It's financial discipleship: learning from someone who's already walked the path successfully.

This isn't cheating—it's strategy. Parents have been adding children to build their credit for decades. Spouses share credit strength through authorized user status. Now you're learning to use this same tool strategically, whether through family, friends, or legitimate tradeline companies.

How Tradelines Transform Your Score Overnight

The Mechanics of Multiplication:

- Someone adds you to their seasoned credit card (2+ years old)
- Their entire payment history appears on YOUR credit report
- Your average account age jumps years instantly
- Your credit mix improves immediately
- Score increases of 50-150 points are common

Real Example: Sarah had a 580 score with two new secured cards. Her aunt added her to a 15-year-old American Express with a $25,000 limit and perfect history. Within 30 days:

- Average account age: From 3 months to 5 years
- Available credit: From $500 to $25,500
- Credit score: 580 to 695

"Two are better than one, because they have a good return for their labor" (Ecclesiastes 4:9). Tradelines are credit partnership in action.

The Three Types of Tradelines

1. Family/Friend Tradelines (Free)

- Most powerful because they're genuine relationships
- Often the longest history and highest limits
- No cost except gratitude and trustworthiness
- Risk: Damaging relationships if mishandled

2. Purchased Tradelines ($500-$2,000)

- Companies like Superior Tradelines, Tradeline Supply
- Temporary (usually 2-3 months active)
- Guaranteed age and limit specifications
- Risk: Expensive and some lenders recognize them

3. Tradeline Exchanges (Trade/Barter)

- Online communities where people swap AU spots
- Medium risk, medium reward
- Requires you have something to offer
- Best for those with mixed credit profiles

The Strategic Tradeline Selection Formula

For Maximum Impact, Choose Tradelines With:

- **Age**: Minimum 2 years, ideally 5+ years
- **Limit**: At least $5,000, ideally $15,000+
- **Utilization**: Under 10% consistently
- **Payment History**: Zero late payments ever
- **Bank**: Major banks report most reliably

"Plans fail for lack of counsel, but with many advisers they succeed" (Proverbs 15:22). Choose your tradeline partners like you choose advisers—carefully.

The Right Way to Request Family Tradelines

The Conversation Script: "[Name], I'm working to rebuild my credit and establish financial stability. I've been making all payments on time for [X] months. Would you consider adding me as an authorized user to one of your older cards? I don't need the physical card—just the credit history help. I'm happy to pay you $[amount] monthly for this blessing."

What to Offer:

- Monthly payment for the privilege
- Written agreement about terms
- Promise not to request the physical card
- Regular updates on your credit progress
- Immediate removal upon request

The Tradeline Timing Strategy

Month 1-3: Build your own foundation first

- Get secured cards reporting
- Establish payment patterns
- Show you're serious

Month 4-6: Add first tradeline

- Start with one to see impact
- Choose oldest available
- Monitor credit reports

Month 7-9: Strategic additions

- Add second if needed
- Focus on different banks
- Watch for diminishing returns

Month 10-12: Maintain and transition

- Keep relationships strong
- Build your own aged accounts

- Graduate to independence

The Ethical & Legal Guidelines
Legal:

- Being added as authorized user ✓
- Paying for tradeline access ✓
- Using to qualify for credit ✓

Illegal:

- Lying about relationships ✗
- Using stolen identities ✗
- Misrepresenting your role ✗

Ethical Considerations:

- Don't abuse family relationships
- Be transparent with lenders if asked
- Use as stepping stone, not permanent crutch
- Pay it forward when you're established

"The integrity of the upright guides them, but the unfaithful are destroyed by their duplicity" (Proverbs 11:3). Use tradelines with integrity, not deception.

Maximizing Your Tradeline Investment
If Purchasing:

- Calculate cost per point gained
- Choose 2-3 strategic lines over many cheap ones
- Time purchases for major credit needs
- Use during mortgage/auto loan applications

If Family/Friend:

- Protect their credit like your own

- Never ask for physical card
- Offer to monitor their account
- Remove yourself when stable

The Exit Strategy

Remember: Tradelines are temporary tools, not permanent solutions. Your goal:

1. Use tradelines to boost score
2. Qualify for your own primary accounts
3. Build your own aged history
4. Become the tradeline others need

"When I was a child, I spoke as a child, I understood as a child, I thought as a child; but when I became a man, I put away childish things" (1 Corinthians 13:11). Tradelines are credit training wheels—powerful for learning, but meant to be outgrown.

Your tradeline strategy should be like Elisha inheriting Elijah's mantle—receiving an anointing that empowers you to eventually walk in your own authority. Use them wisely, gratefully, and temporarily as you build your own credit legacy.

***

Section 1: Tradeline Vendors & Primary Account Builders - Your Strategic Arsenal

The Vendor Landscape: Choosing Your Credit Allies

"Where there is no guidance, a people falls, but in an abundance of counselors there is safety" (Proverbs 11:14).

Not all tradeline vendors are created equal. Some are modern-day money changers in the temple, while others operate with integrity to help people rebuild. Here's your vetted list of legitimate players who can accelerate your credit resurrection when used strategically.

Tradeline Supply: The Industry Standard

What They Offer:

- Authorized user tradelines from $300-$3,000
- Ages ranging from 2-20+ years
- Limits from $5,000-$50,000+
- Two-month guarantee period

Selection Strategy:

- **Excellent Payment History:** Only choose cards with 100% on-time payments
- **Credit Utilization:** Must be under 15% (ideally under 10%)
- **Amazing Age:** Minimum 5 years for real impact, 10+ years for maximum boost

The $1,500 Sweet Spot: Their tradelines around this price point often give the best cost-per-point improvement—typically 10+ years old with $20,000+ limits.

"Buy truth, and do not sell it; buy wisdom, instruction, and understanding" (Proverbs 23:23). Quality tradelines are an investment in your financial wisdom journey.

Credit Strong: The $20,000 Magnum Primary Tradeline

This isn't a traditional tradeline—it's a revolutionary primary account builder:

The Magnum Account:

- $1,000 monthly payments into locked savings
- Builds massive payment history fast
- Shows ability to handle large obligations
- Creates both installment AND revolving history

Strategic Deployment:

- Only for those with $20,000 liquid to lock up
- Best used 6-12 months before major purchase (home)
- Shows lenders you can handle mortgage-level payments
- Graduates to accessible funds after completion

The Alternative Primary Builders

Ava Credit Cards ($2,500):

- Virtual card for online purchases
- No credit check approval
- Reports as primary tradeline
- Builds payment history from day one

Stellefy Installment Loans (Up to $25,000):

- Designed for thin credit files
- Uses alternative data for approval
- Reports to all three bureaus
- Interest rates reflect risk (expect 15-30%)

Warning: *"The borrower is slave to the lender" (Proverbs 22:7).* These tools build credit but at a cost. Calculate if the credit gain justifies the interest paid.

Business Credit: The Second Credit File

Global Voice Direct Business Toll-Free Line ($7,500):

- Establishes business credit profile
- Reports to Dun & Bradstreet
- No personal guarantee required
- Creates separation between personal/business

How It Works:

1. Get business phone line
2. They report your payment history
3. Build business credit score
4. Access business funding without personal credit

Your Vendor Selection Matrix
For Authorized User Tradelines:

- Budget under $1,000: Focus on age over limit
- Budget $1,000-$2,000: Balance age and limit
- Budget over $2,000: Maximum age AND limit

For Primary Accounts:

- Income under $50k: Start with **Ava** or **secured cards**
- Income $50k-$100k: Consider **Stellefy** or small **Credit Strong**
- Income over $100k: Magnum account viable option

The Strategic Sequencing
Month 1: Foundation

- Research and verify vendors
- Calculate total investment needed
- Set aside funds

Month 2-3: Authorized User Phase

- Add 1-2 quality tradelines
- Monitor reporting accuracy

- Document score changes

Month 4-6: Primary Account Phase

- Add Credit Strong or alternative
- Establish payment patterns
- Build relationship history

Month 7-12: Optimization

- Maintain all accounts perfectly
- Request limit increases
- Prepare for graduation to traditional credit

The Risk Management Protocol

"The prudent see danger and take refuge, but the simple keep going and pay the penalty" (Proverbs 27:12).

Before Purchasing Any Tradeline:

- Verify company BBB rating and reviews
- Confirm money-back guarantees
- Get reporting timeline in writing
- Never wire money—use credit cards for protection
- Screenshot everything before purchase

Red Flags to Avoid:

- Promises of specific point increases
- Requirements to lie to lenders
- No physical address or phone
- Prices too good to be true
- Pressure to buy immediately

Your Investment Recovery Plan

Every dollar spent on tradelines should return multiplied:

- $1,500 tradeline → 100-point increase → $5,000 saved on car loan
- $20,000 Credit Strong → Mortgage approval → $50,000 saved in interest
- $7,500 business line → $100,000 business credit access

Remember: *"Cast your bread upon the waters, for after many days you will find it again" (Ecclesiastes 11:1).* Strategic credit building investments return exponentially when deployed wisely. These aren't expenses—they're seeds for your financial harvest.

Choose vendors like you choose ministry partners: carefully, prayerfully, and with clear expectations of fruit.

***

Section 2: The Most Trusted Tradeline Vendors - A Comprehensive Review

The Reputation Leaders in Authorized User Tradelines

"A good name is to be chosen rather than great riches, and favor is better than silver or gold" (Proverbs 22:1).

After years of market testing and thousands of customer reviews, certain tradeline vendors have risen above the rest. These companies have built reputations on consistent delivery, ethical practices, and genuine results. Here's your detailed guide to the most recommended vendors in the industry.

Tradeline Supply Company - The Gold Standard

Why They're #1: Operating since 2010, Tradeline Supply Company has become the most recognized name in the industry with an A+ BBB rating and over 10,000 successful customers.

What Sets Them Apart:

- **Transparent Pricing**: Every tradeline shows exact age, limit, and bank
- **Two-Month Guarantee**: Full refund if line doesn't post
- **Educational Resources**: Free guides on maximizing tradeline impact
- **No Hidden Fees**: Price you see is price you pay

Customer Favorite Tradelines:

- Bank of America 15+ years, $25,000 limit ($1,500-$1,800)
- Chase 10+ years, $15,000 limit ($1,200-$1,400)
- Discover 8+ years, $10,000 limit ($800-$1,000)

Real User Testimony: "Added their 12-year BOA line, score went from 620 to 718 in 35 days. Used the boost to get approved for my first mortgage." - Marcus T.

Superior Tradelines - The Customer Service Champion

Why They're Loved: Known for hand-holding first-time buyers through the process with unlimited phone support and personal account managers.

Unique Features:

- **Score Simulator:** Predicts your specific point increase
- **Package Deals:** Buy 2+ lines for 20% discount
- **Extended Posting:** Some lines stay active 3-4 months
- **Spouse Discounts:** 50% off for married couples

Best Sellers:

- Wells Fargo 20+ years, $30,000 limit ($2,200)
- Capital One 12+ years, $20,000 limit ($1,400)
- Citi 10+ years, $15,000 limit ($1,100)

"Iron sharpens iron, and one man sharpens another" (Proverbs 27:17). Their customer service team truly sharpens your understanding of credit building.

BoostMyScore - The Fast-Track Specialists

Their Niche: Specializing in rapid posting for time-sensitive needs like mortgage applications or job opportunities requiring credit checks.

Speed Advantages:

- **7-Day Posting:** Fastest in industry (most take 15-30 days)
- **Rush Options:** 3-day emergency posting available
- **Pre-Approval:** Know if you qualify before paying
- **Multiple Bureau Reporting:** Ensures all three bureaus update

Popular Quick-Post Lines:

- Amex Gold 8+ years, $25,000 limit ($1,600)
- US Bank 10+ years, $12,000 limit ($1,000)
- Navy Federal 15+ years, $20,000 limit ($1,800)

Personal Tradelines - The Budget-Friendly Option

Why Consider Them: Lower prices without sacrificing quality, perfect for those needing multiple lines on a budget.

Cost-Saving Features:

- **Bulk Pricing**: 3+ lines get 30% discount
- **Loyalty Program**: Returning customers save 15%
- **Payment Plans**: Split cost over 2-3 months
- **Referral Rewards**: $100 credit per referral

Best Value Lines:

- Regional banks 5+ years, $5,000 limit ($400-$600)
- Credit unions 8+ years, $8,000 limit ($600-$800)
- Store cards 10+ years, $10,000 limit ($500-$700)

The Vendor Verification Checklist

"Test everything; hold fast what is good" (1 Thessalonians 5:21).

Before purchasing from ANY vendor:

Must-Have Credentials:

- [ ] BBB accreditation with A rating minimum
- [ ] Physical business address (not just PO Box)
- [ ] Clear refund policy in writing
- [ ] Secure payment processing
- [ ] Customer service phone number
- [ ] Online reviews across multiple platforms

Red Flag Warnings:

- "Guaranteed 100+ point increase" (impossible to promise)
- "Primary tradelines for sale" (illegal)
- "No refunds under any circumstances"
- Requires cryptocurrency only
- No company history before 2020

Maximizing Your Vendor Experience
Best Practices for Success:

1. **Start Communication Early**
    - Email questions before purchasing
    - Test their response time
    - Judge their knowledge level
2. **Document Everything**
    - Screenshot tradeline details before purchase
    - Save all email correspondence
    - Keep payment receipts
    - Monitor your credit reports weekly
3. **Time Your Purchase**
    - Buy 45-60 days before major credit need
    - Avoid holiday seasons (slower posting)
    - Tuesday-Thursday purchases post fastest

The Cost-Benefit Analysis
Typical Investment Returns:

- $1,000 tradeline → 80-point increase → Save $8,000 on auto loan
- $1,500 tradeline → 100-point increase → Qualify for rewards cards
- $2,000 tradeline → 120-point increase → Save $40,000 on mortgage

Remember: *"For which of you, desiring to build a tower, does not first sit down and count the cost?" (Luke 14:28).* Calculate your potential savings before investing. A quality tradeline from a reputable vendor isn't an expense—it's an investment that pays dividends through lower interest rates and better opportunities.

Choose vendors who operate in the light, provide clear terms, and have proven track records. Your financial resurrection deserves partners who match your commitment to integrity and transformation.

***

Section 3: Authorized User vs. Primary Tradelines – Understanding the Difference That Builds Destiny

Two Paths to Credit Resurrection

"Wisdom is the principal thing; therefore get wisdom: and with all thy getting get understanding" (Proverbs 4:7).

When rebuilding credit, two powerful tools stand before you: authorized user tradelines and primary tradelines. Both can elevate your score, but they do so in fundamentally different ways. Understanding the distinction is not just financial—it's spiritual. One path borrows credibility; the other builds it. One is inherited favor; the other is earned authority.

Let's break down the difference and explore how each can serve your journey toward financial restoration and legacy.

Authorized User Tradelines: Borrowed Favor

"And the Lord said to Joshua, 'Today I will begin to exalt you in the eyes of all Israel, so they may know that I am with you as I was with Moses'" (Joshua 3:7).

Becoming an authorized user is like stepping into someone else's credit covenant. You're added to their account, and their payment history, age, and utilization become part of your credit report. You don't own the account, but you benefit from its reputation.

Benefits of Authorized User Tradelines:

- Immediate score boost (often 50–100 points)
- No credit check or income verification
- Ideal for thin or new credit files
- Can be free if added by family or friends

Limitations:

- You're not legally responsible for the debt
- Some lenders discount AU history when underwriting
- If the account holder mismanages the card, your score suffers

- It's temporary—meant to be a bridge, not a foundation

This is favor in action. Like Ruth gleaning in Boaz's field, you're reaping from someone else's harvest. It's a powerful tool—but it's not the full inheritance.

Primary Tradelines: Built Authority

"By wisdom a house is built, and through understanding it is established; through knowledge its rooms are filled with rare and beautiful treasures" (Proverbs 24:3–4).

Primary tradelines are accounts you own. You applied, you were approved, and you're responsible for the payments. These include secured credit cards, credit builder loans, auto loans, and personal lines of credit. They carry more weight with lenders because they reflect your financial behavior—not someone else's.

Benefits of Primary Tradelines:

- Full control and responsibility
- Stronger impact on creditworthiness
- Required for major approvals (mortgages, business credit)
- Builds long-term financial credibility

Limitations:

- Requires income and credit evaluation
- May involve deposits or higher interest rates
- Takes time to build age and payment history

Primary tradelines are your financial testimony. They prove you can steward resources, honor agreements, and grow in discipline. They're not borrowed—they're built.

Strategic Comparison

Feature	Authorized User Tradeline	Primary Tradeline
Ownership	No	Yes
Responsibility	None	Full
Impact on Score	Moderate to High	High
Lender Weight	Low to Moderate	High
Setup Speed	Fast	Moderate
Long-Term Value	Temporary	Permanent
Risk Level	Depends on account holder	Depends on your discipline

"The wise man built his house upon the rock" (Matthew 7:24). Primary tradelines are the rock. Authorized user tradelines are scaffolding—they help you build, but they're not the structure.

How to Use Both Strategically

Step 1: Start with 1–2 authorized user tradelines to boost your score quickly

Step 2: Open secured credit cards and credit builder loans to establish primary history

Step 3: Maintain perfect payment history and low utilization

Step 4: Graduate to unsecured cards and auto loans

Step 5: Remove AU accounts once your own history is strong

This layered strategy allows you to benefit from favor while building your own authority. It's the same principle God used with Joshua—He honored him like Moses, but Joshua still had to fight his own battles.

The Kingdom Perspective

Authorized user tradelines reflect grace—unearned favor that lifts you up. Primary tradelines reflect stewardship—earned trust that multiplies over time. Both are biblical. Both are powerful. But only one builds legacy.

"If you are faithful with little, you will be trusted with much" (Luke 16:10). Authorized user status may open the door, but primary tradelines prove you're ready to walk through it.

Use both wisely. Build with intention. And let your credit journey reflect the restoration, wisdom, and favor of God.

***

Section 4: How the Wealthy Use Aged Accounts to Qualify for Funding – The Strategy of Seasoned Stewardship

The Power of Credit Age in Unlocking Capital

"The plans of the diligent lead surely to abundance, but everyone who is hasty comes only to poverty" (Proverbs 21:5).

When it comes to qualifying for high-limit funding, the wealthy don't rely on luck or last-minute applications—they rely on aged accounts. These are credit lines, loans, and revolving accounts that have been open for years, maintained with perfect payment history, and kept at low utilization. The age of an account is one of the most powerful indicators of financial stability, and lenders treat it like gold.

Credit age reflects consistency, discipline, and trustworthiness. It shows that the borrower has weathered financial seasons without defaulting. The wealthy understand this principle and intentionally cultivate aged accounts long before they need funding. They don't wait until they need capital—they prepare for it in advance.

What Is an Aged Account?

An aged account is any credit line that has been open for several years—typically five years or more—with a spotless payment history. These accounts may be:

- Credit cards with high limits and low balances
- Installment loans paid down over time
- Business lines of credit with consistent usage
- Authorized user tradelines with long histories

The longer the account has been open and active, the more weight it carries in underwriting decisions. Lenders view aged accounts as proof of financial maturity.

"Even to your old age and gray hairs I am he, I am he who will sustain you" (Isaiah 46:4). In the credit world, age sustains your score and opens doors to favor.

Why Lenders Love Aged Accounts

Lenders use aged accounts to assess risk. A borrower with multiple accounts over 5–10 years old is seen as stable, predictable, and low-risk. This translates into:

- Higher approval rates
- Lower interest rates
- Larger funding amounts
- Faster underwriting decisions

Wealthy individuals often maintain aged accounts with minimal activity, just to preserve the age and history. They understand that every month of perfect reporting adds value—even if they don't need the credit today.

"By wisdom a house is built, and through understanding it is established" (Proverbs 24:3). Aged accounts are the bricks of financial wisdom—laid over time, not overnight.

Strategic Uses of Aged Accounts

1. Business Funding Before applying for business credit, the wealthy ensure their personal credit profile includes aged accounts. This boosts their credibility and allows them to qualify for:

- $50,000–$250,000 unsecured business lines
- SBA loans with favorable terms
- Vendor credit with net-30 or net-60 terms

2. Real Estate Financing Mortgage lenders heavily weigh credit age. A borrower with aged accounts can:

- Secure lower down payments
- Qualify for jumbo loans
- Avoid private mortgage insurance (PMI)

3. High-Limit Credit Cards Premium cards like the Amex Platinum or Chase Sapphire Reserve often require aged accounts. These cards offer:

- Travel rewards

- Concierge services
- Purchase protections
- Status-based perks

4. Personal Loans and Refinancing Aged accounts help qualify for personal loans with:

- Fixed rates under 10%
- Terms up to 7 years
- No collateral required

How the Wealthy Build Aged Accounts Intentionally

Start Early, Use Lightly They open accounts in their teens or early twenties and keep them open for decades. Even if the card is rarely used, it remains active and reporting.

Avoid Closing Accounts Closing old accounts shortens credit age. The wealthy keep accounts open—even if unused—to preserve their score.

Add Authorized Users They add children or spouses to aged accounts to pass on credit history. This builds generational credit strength.

Use Business Credit Separately They build aged business accounts to protect personal credit age. This creates two strong profiles—personal and business.

"A good man leaves an inheritance to his children's children" (Proverbs 13:22). Aged accounts are part of that inheritance—financial credibility passed down through wisdom.

Your Action Plan to Build Aged Accounts

Step 1: Open secured cards and credit builder loans now

Step 2: Keep utilization under 10% and automate payments

Step 3: Never close accounts with positive history

Step 4: Add authorized users to your oldest accounts

Step 5: Monitor your credit age monthly and protect it like a legacy

Remember: You don't build aged accounts in a hurry. You build them with intention, consistency, and patience. The wealthy understand that time is a multiplier—and aged accounts are the proof.

"Let us not grow weary in doing good, for at the proper time we will reap a harvest if we do not give up" (Galatians 6:9). Your aged accounts are seeds. Water them with discipline, protect them with wisdom, and watch them unlock the harvest of funding, favor, and financial freedom.

***

Section 5: Risks, Ethics, and How to Do It Right – Building Credit with Integrity

The Temptation to Cut Corners

"There is a way that seems right to a man, but its end is the way to death" (Proverbs 14:12).

In the world of credit repair and financial rebuilding, shortcuts are everywhere. From shady tradeline vendors to deceptive credit sweeps, consumers are often lured into quick fixes that promise instant results but carry long-term consequences. The temptation to manipulate the system, hide the truth, or exploit loopholes is real—but it's not righteous.

God's Word calls us to build with integrity, not just effectiveness. A high credit score gained through deception is a fragile foundation. True financial restoration must be rooted in truth, stewardship, and wisdom. The goal is not just approval—it's legacy.

Common Risks in Credit Repair

1. Fraudulent Tradeline Vendors Some companies sell "primary tradelines" that are actually fabricated or illegally obtained. Purchasing these can result in:

- Account closures
- Credit score reversals
- Legal consequences

2. Credit Sweeps and False Disputes Credit sweeps involve disputing all negative items as "identity theft," even when they're legitimate. This tactic may temporarily remove items, but once verified, they return—and often with penalties.

3. Misuse of Authorized User Status Adding someone to your credit card without their knowledge, or being added to a card with poor payment history, can damage both parties. Lenders may also discount AU accounts if they suspect manipulation.

4. Overleveraging Installment Loans Stacking too many credit builder loans or secured cards without the income to support them can lead to missed payments, high utilization, and score drops.

"The integrity of the upright guides them, but the crookedness of the treacherous destroys them" (Proverbs 11:3). Integrity protects your progress. Deception destroys it.

Ethical Credit Building Principles

1. Transparency Always be honest with lenders, vendors, and yourself. If you're rebuilding, say so. Many institutions offer second-chance programs for those who are upfront.

2. Stewardship Don't open accounts you can't manage. Credit is a tool, not a trophy. Use it to build, not to impress.

3. Consent and Communication If you're adding someone as an authorized user, get their full consent. If you're being added, understand the risks. This is a financial covenant—treat it with respect.

4. Patience Over Pressure Avoid rushing into credit decisions out of desperation. Take time to research, pray, and plan. The right opportunity will align with peace, not panic.

"Better is a poor man who walks in his integrity than a rich man who is crooked in his ways" (Proverbs 28:6). Your credit journey should reflect your character, not just your goals.

How to Do It Right: The Righteous Blueprint

Step 1: Start with Truth Pull your credit reports from all three bureaus. Review every item honestly. Dispute only what is truly inaccurate.

Step 2: Build with Wisdom Open 2–3 secured cards with manageable deposits. Add one credit builder loan. Keep utilization under 10%. Automate payments.

Step 3: Use Tradelines Strategically Only purchase authorized user tradelines from verified vendors. Choose accounts with perfect history, low utilization, and long age. Never pay for primary tradelines that aren't truly yours.

Step 4: Monitor and Maintain Check your credit monthly. Track your score, payment history, and utilization. Adjust as needed. Celebrate progress, not perfection.

Step 5: Teach Others Once you've rebuilt, share your testimony. Help others avoid the traps you escaped. Your breakthrough becomes someone else's blueprint.

"Let your light so shine before men, that they may see your good works and glorify your Father in heaven" (Matthew 5:16). Ethical credit building isn't just financial—it's ministry. It shows the world that restoration is possible, and righteousness still works.

Final Word: Build to Last

Quick fixes fade. Integrity endures. The risks of deception are real, but so are the rewards of doing it right. When you build your credit with truth, patience, and wisdom, you're not just raising your score—you're raising your standard.

Let your financial resurrection reflect the glory of God. Let your credit report become a testimony of stewardship, discipline, and divine favor. And let every account you open be a covenant of trust, not a compromise of truth.

***

Section 6: Foundations of Credit Resurrection – Secured Cards, Credit-Builder Loans, Rent Reporting, and Authorized User Strategies

Building Credit from the Ground Up

"Unless the Lord builds the house, the builders labor in vain" (Psalm 127:1).

Credit restoration begins with structure. Before you qualify for high-limit cards or business funding, you must lay a foundation of trust, consistency, and stewardship. Chapter 4 introduces the four pillars of credit resurrection—secured cards, credit-builder loans, rent reporting, and authorized user strategies. These tools are accessible, ethical, and powerful when used with wisdom. They don't just rebuild your score—they rebuild your testimony.

Secured Cards – The First Step Toward Trust

"Whoever can be trusted with very little can also be trusted with much" (Luke 16:10).

Secured credit cards are the training ground for financial discipline. You deposit your own money—typically $200 to $1,000—and the bank issues a credit card backed by that deposit. Every on-time payment is reported to the credit bureaus, proving your reliability.

Why It Works:

- Builds revolving credit history
- Reports monthly to all three bureaus
- Graduates to unsecured after 6–12 months
- Often comes with rewards and credit limit increases

Strategy:

- Use only 1–3% of your limit monthly
- Automate payments
- Request graduation after 6 months

This is your "yes" in the small things. It's not about the limit—it's about the legacy you're building through consistency.

Credit-Builder Loans – Installment History Without Risk

"The plans of the diligent lead surely to abundance" (Proverbs 21:5).

Credit-builder loans are installment loans where the bank holds the funds in a savings account while you make monthly payments. Once the loan is paid off, you receive the money—and a perfect payment history.

Benefits:

- Adds installment loan history
- Builds savings while building credit
- Reports monthly to all bureaus
- Can be stacked for greater impact

Strategy:

- Start with $300–$1,000 loan
- Choose 12–24 month term
- Automate payments
- Track progress monthly

This tool reflects biblical stewardship—paying faithfully, saving wisely, and reaping a harvest in due time.

Rent Reporting – Turning Your Home into a Credit Asset

"By wisdom a house is built, and through understanding it is established" (Proverbs 24:3).

Most people pay rent for years without realizing it can build credit. Rent reporting services allow you to report your monthly rent payments to the credit bureaus, adding positive history without taking on new debt.

Top Rent Reporting Services:

- RentReporters
- Esusu
- Piñata
- CreditMyRent

Why It Matters:

- Adds tradeline with 12–24 months of history
- Boosts score for thin files
- Reflects real-world responsibility

Strategy:

- Choose a service that reports to all three bureaus
- Backdate up to 24 months if possible
- Ensure landlord verification is smooth

Rent reporting turns your roof into a resource. It's proof that you've been faithful—even when no one was watching.

Authorized User Strategies – Borrowing Favor to Build Faith

"Two are better than one, because they have a good return for their labor" (Ecclesiastes 4:9).

Being added as an authorized user to someone else's seasoned credit card allows you to inherit their payment history, age, and limit. It's a legal and ethical way to boost your score—especially when your own credit is thin or damaged.

Best Practices:

- Choose cards with 5+ years of history
- Ensure utilization is under 10%
- Never request the physical card
- Remove yourself once your own credit is strong

Who to Ask:

- Parents
- Spouses
- Trusted friends
- Mentors

This is borrowed favor—like Ruth gleaning in Boaz's field. It's not permanent, but it's powerful when used with humility and gratitude.

Final Word: Build with Wisdom, Not Haste

These four tools—secured cards, credit-builder loans, rent reporting, and authorized user strategies—form the foundation of your credit resurrection. They are simple, accessible, and proven. But they require discipline, patience, and integrity.

"Do not despise these small beginnings, for the Lord rejoices to see the work begin" (Zechariah 4:10). Your credit journey may start small, but it's sacred. Every payment is a seed. Every report is a testimony. Every strategy is a step toward restoration.

Build wisely. Steward faithfully. And let your credit profile reflect the glory of a life rebuilt by grace and guided by truth.

Chapter 6: Score Boosting Tools the Banks Don't Advertise – Hidden Keys to Financial Favor

The Secret Weapons Hidden in Plain Sight

"It is the glory of God to conceal a matter; to search out a matter is the glory of kings" (Proverbs 25:2).

Banks and credit unions offer powerful tools that can dramatically boost your credit score—but they rarely advertise them. These hidden resources are often tucked away in the fine print, reserved for those who ask, research, or are guided by financial wisdom. The wealthy and well-informed use these tools to unlock funding, qualify for elite credit products, and build generational wealth. Now, you can too.

This chapter reveals the score-boosting strategies banks don't promote publicly, but that can transform your credit profile when used with diligence and discernment.

1. Credit Builder Loans (Hidden in the Loan Department)

Most banks offer credit builder loans, but they're not listed on the homepage or promoted in ads. These loans don't give you money upfront—instead, they hold the funds in a savings account while you make monthly payments. Once the loan is paid off, you receive the funds and a perfect payment history.

Why It Works:

- Builds installment loan history
- Adds 12–24 months of on-time payments
- Improves credit mix (30% of your score)

"The wise store up knowledge, but the mouth of a fool invites ruin" (Proverbs 10:14). Credit builder loans are knowledge-based tools—those who seek them find favor.

2. Secured Cards That Graduate

Many banks offer secured credit cards that automatically convert to unsecured after 6–12 months of perfect payments. These cards often come with:

- No annual fee
- Rewards points
- Credit limit increases

Examples:

- Discover it® Secured
- Capital One Secured Mastercard
- Apple FCU Secured Visa®

Graduation means your deposit is returned, your limit increases, and your score jumps due to improved utilization and account age.

"Whoever can be trusted with very little can also be trusted with much" (Luke 16:10). These cards test your stewardship before granting greater access.

3. Soft-Pull Credit Limit Increases

Some banks allow you to request credit limit increases without a hard inquiry. This boosts your available credit, lowers your utilization, and improves your score—without damaging your report.

Banks That Offer Soft-Pull Increases:

- Capital One
- Discover
- Navy Federal Credit Union
- Synchrony Bank (Amazon, PayPal, etc.)

Strategy:

- Request every 6 months
- Keep utilization under 10%
- Use card monthly, pay in full before statement date

"Ask, and it will be given to you; seek, and you will find" (Matthew 7:7). Many don't receive because they don't ask—soft-pull increases are granted to the diligent.

4. Authorized User Tradelines (Quietly Accepted)

While banks don't promote this, most allow you to add authorized users to your credit cards. When added to a seasoned account, the user inherits the card's age, limit, and payment history.

Best Practices:

- Choose cards with 5+ years of history
- Keep utilization under 10%
- Never request the physical card
- Remove yourself once your own credit is strong

"Two are better than one, because they have a good return for their labor" (Ecclesiastes 4:9). Authorized user status is a partnership that multiplies favor.

5. Business Secured Credit Cards

Business credit cards don't report to personal credit unless you default. This allows you to build a second credit profile while protecting your personal score.

Banks That Offer Business Secured Cards:

- Wells Fargo
- Bank of America
- Capital One Spark
- Nav (via partner banks)

Benefits:

- Builds business credit
- Separates personal and business finances
- Can be used to qualify for business funding

"Enlarge the place of your tent, stretch your tent curtains wide, do not hold back" (Isaiah 54:2). Business credit is expansion—don't limit yourself to personal accounts.

6. Skip-a-Pay Programs

Many credit unions and banks offer "skip-a-pay" options once per year. This allows you to skip a loan payment without penalty or damage to your credit.

Use Cases:

- Emergency cash flow
- Avoiding late payments
- Preserving perfect history

Institutions That Offer It:

- Apple FCU
- Navy Federal
- Digital Federal Credit Union
- Local credit unions

"The Lord is gracious and compassionate, slow to anger and rich in love" (Psalm 145:8). Skip-a-pay programs reflect grace in the financial system—use them wisely.

7. Early Graduation from Secured Products

Some banks allow early graduation from secured cards or loans if you demonstrate perfect payment history and low utilization. You must ask—this is rarely automatic.

How to Request:

- Call customer service after 6 months
- Ask for "product change to unsecured"
- Request without hard inquiry
- Document approval and new terms

"You have not because you ask not" (James 4:2). Early graduation is available to those who ask boldly and steward faithfully.

Final Word: Steward the Secrets

These tools are not hidden from you—they're hidden for you. They require diligence, wisdom, and intentionality to uncover. The banks don't advertise them because they're reserved for those who build with strategy, not impulse.

"The secret of the Lord is with those who fear Him, and He will show them His covenant" (Psalm 25:14). These score-boosting tools are part of your covenant of restoration. Use them with integrity, and watch your credit profile become a testimony of favor, wisdom, and breakthrough.

***

Section 1: Business Credit Hack – How to Secure $150,000 at 0% Interest Without Income Proof

The Strategy of Faith-Fueled Leverage

"Enlarge the place of your tent, stretch your tent curtains wide, do not hold back; lengthen your cords, strengthen your stakes" (Isaiah 54:2).

In the Kingdom economy, expansion often begins with obedience and strategy—not excess. The same is true in business credit. You don't need six figures in income to access six figures in funding. You need structure, stewardship, and strategic leverage. This business credit hack reveals how everyday entrepreneurs can secure up to $150,000 in 0% interest credit—without showing income—by using legal, ethical tools banks rarely explain.

This isn't manipulation. It's multiplication. It's the kind of wisdom Joseph used to store grain in Egypt before the famine. It's the kind of favor Nehemiah received when the king funded his rebuilding project. It's the kind of strategy that turns vision into velocity.

Step 1: Form an LLC – Establish Your Business Identity

"Write the vision and make it plain on tablets, that he may run who reads it" (Habakkuk 2:2).

The first step is forming a Limited Liability Company (LLC). This creates a separate legal entity that can apply for credit independently. You don't need revenue yet—just a registered business name, EIN (Employer Identification Number), and business checking account.

Why It Matters:

- Banks lend to entities, not just individuals
- LLCs can apply for business credit without personal income
- You protect your personal assets while building business credibility

This is your foundation. Like laying the cornerstone of a temple, it sets the stage for everything that follows.

Step 2: Leverage Your Personal Credit – Co-Sign with Wisdom

"Whoever walks with the wise becomes wise, but the companion of fools will suffer harm" (Proverbs 13:20).

Even though your business is new, your personal credit history can be used to co-sign or personally guarantee business credit cards. This doesn't mean you're liable for misuse—it means you're vouching for your business's integrity.

Requirements:

- Personal credit score of 680+
- Low utilization (under 10%)
- No recent late payments or derogatory marks

Why It Works:

- Banks trust your personal credit more than your business's age
- You gain access to high-limit cards with 0% interest offers
- You build business credit while protecting your personal score

This is strategic alignment—your personal credibility becomes a bridge to business favor.

Step 3: Apply for 0% Interest Business Credit Cards

"You shall lend to many nations, but you shall not borrow" (Deuteronomy 15:6).

Now comes the harvest. With your LLC formed and personal credit leveraged, you can apply for top-tier business credit cards that offer 0% interest for 12–18 months. These cards allow you to fund inventory, marketing, equipment, or expansion—without paying interest.

Recommended Cards:

- **Chase Ink Business Unlimited®**: 0% APR for 12 months, $15,000–$50,000 limits
- **U.S. Bank Business Platinum**: 0% APR for 18 months, generous approvals
- **American Express Blue Business Cash™**: 0% APR for 12 months, flexible spending limits

Strategy:

- Apply within 30 days of forming your LLC
- Use EIN and business address
- List estimated revenue (not verified)
- Use personal credit as guarantor

These cards are your financial tools—like David's sling, they may seem small, but they carry giant-slaying power.

Step 4: Stack and Multiply – Reach $150,000 in Funding

"To one he gave five talents, to another two, to another one—to each according to his ability" (Matthew 25:15).

By applying to multiple banks strategically, you can stack approvals and reach $150,000 in total credit. Each bank evaluates your application independently, and business credit inquiries don't impact your personal score the same way.

Stacking Tips:

- Space applications 3–5 days apart
- Start with banks that pull from different bureaus (e.g., Chase = Experian, US Bank = TransUnion)
- Use approved cards for business expenses only
- Track utilization and payment dates carefully

This is stewardship in action—multiplying what you've been given through wisdom, timing, and discipline.

Final Word: Build with Integrity, Expand with Faith

This strategy isn't just about funding—it's about freedom. It's about using what you have to build what you've been called to create. It's about accessing resources without compromising righteousness.

"Commit your works to the Lord, and your plans will be established" (Proverbs 16:3).

Form your LLC. Leverage your credit. Apply with wisdom. And build your business with the confidence that Heaven backs your vision. ***

Section 2: Business credit cards that use only your EIN (Employer Identification Number) instead of your Social Security Number are designed to help entrepreneurs build credit under their business entity, not their personal name. Each issuer has different requirements, and understanding them is key to accessing funding while protecting your personal credit.

Chapter 19: Business Credit Cards by EIN – Building with Strategy, Not Strain

Build the House Without Burdening the Builder

"Unless the Lord builds the house, the builders labor in vain..." (Psalm 127:1).

God calls us to build with wisdom, not weariness. For entrepreneurs and small business owners, using business credit cards tied to an EIN instead of a Social Security Number is a strategic way to access funding, protect personal credit, and establish financial credibility. These cards allow your business to stand on its own merit—just as God equips each calling with its own provision.

Let's explore what's required for each card and how they align with the principle of stewardship.

EIN-Only Business Credit Cards – What You Need

"The borrower is slave to the lender" (Proverbs 22:7).

True EIN-only cards typically require:

A legally formed business (LLC, corporation)

An EIN from the IRS

A business bank account

Strong revenue or cash flow

A DUNS number and business credit profile

These cards do not require a personal credit check or guarantee. They reflect financial maturity—your business is seen as creditworthy on its own.

Valley Business Credit Cards

Valley Bank offers business credit cards that may allow EIN-only applications for established businesses. Requirements include:

Business registration and EIN

Business bank account with Valley

Financial statements or tax returns

This card is ideal for regional businesses seeking relationship-based banking. Stewardship begins with local trust.

Hello Alice Business Credit Cards

Hello Alice partners with Mastercard to offer small business credit cards focused on underserved entrepreneurs. Requirements:

EIN and

Hello Alice Business Credit Cards

"Enlarge the place of your tent... do not hold back; lengthen your cords, strengthen your stakes" (Isaiah 54:2).

Hello Alice partners with Mastercard to offer business credit cards tailored to small businesses and underserved entrepreneurs. While they do request basic business information, they emphasize inclusive underwriting and may consider EIN-only applications for established entities.

Requirements:

- EIN and legal business entity (LLC or corporation)
- Business bank account
- Revenue documentation or business plan
- May still request SSN for identity verification, but not for credit pull

This card is ideal for mission-driven entrepreneurs seeking funding aligned with purpose and impact.

FNBO Business Credit Cards

"The Lord will open the heavens, the storehouse of His bounty, to bless all the work of your hands" (Deuteronomy 28:12).

First National Bank of Omaha (FNBO) offers business credit cards that may allow EIN-only applications for businesses with strong financials. They are known for conservative underwriting, so having a solid business credit profile is key.

Requirements:

- EIN and legal entity
- Business credit history (DUNS number recommended)
- Business bank account and financials

- May require personal guarantee if business credit is thin

FNBO reflects the principle of diligence—rewarding those who build with consistency and clarity.

Tillful Business Credit Cards

"The prudent see danger and take refuge..." (Proverbs 27:12).

Tillful offers business credit cards and credit-building tools specifically designed for EIN-only use. They focus on alternative data and business performance rather than personal credit scores.

Requirements:

- EIN and registered business
- Business bank account
- Revenue or cash flow history
- No personal credit check required

Tillful is a modern-day example of redemptive finance—giving access to those rebuilding or starting fresh.

Bank of America Advantage Business Credit Cards

"Commit your works to the Lord, and your plans will be established" (Proverbs 16:3).

Bank of America offers several business credit cards under the "Advantage" brand. While most require a personal guarantee, established businesses with strong EIN-based credit may qualify for limited EIN-only options.

Requirements:

- EIN and legal entity
- Business bank account with Bank of America
- Strong revenue and business credit history
- May still request SSN for verification

This card is best for businesses with existing relationships and financial strength.

Capital One Spark Business Credit Cards

"He who had received five talents went at once and traded with them..." (Matthew 25:16).

Capital One Spark cards are popular among entrepreneurs, but they typically require a personal credit check—even if you apply with an EIN. However, they report to both personal and business credit bureaus, which can help build both profiles.

Requirements:

- EIN and legal entity
- SSN for credit check
- Business bank account
- Revenue documentation

While not truly EIN-only, Spark cards can be a stepping stone toward full business credit independence.

Suncoast Business Credit Card

"The Lord is my shepherd, I lack nothing" (Psalm 23:1).

Suncoast Credit Union offers business credit cards to Florida-based businesses. They prioritize relationship banking and may offer EIN-only options for well-established entities.

Requirements:

- EIN and Florida-registered business
- Business bank account with Suncoast
- Financial statements or tax returns
- May require SSN for identity verification

This card is ideal for local entrepreneurs seeking community-based funding with personalized support.

Final Word: Build Credit with Wisdom, Not Worry

"Through wisdom a house is built, and by understanding it is established" (Proverbs 24:3).

Business credit cards tied to your EIN are tools of multiplication, not manipulation. They allow you to build without burdening your personal credit, access funding for growth, and position your business for legacy. Each issuer has its own requirements, but the principle remains: structure unlocks stewardship.

Start with one. Build your profile. Use it wisely. And let your business reflect the order, favor, and financial authority of the Kingdom.

***

Section 3: Continued: Getting Loans with Poor Credit – Wisdom, Strategy, and Protection

The Reality of Borrowing While Rebuilding

"The borrower is slave to the lender" (Proverbs 22:7).

When your credit is damaged, borrowing money can feel like walking through a minefield. The need is real—emergencies arise, opportunities knock, and sometimes rebuilding requires access to capital. But without discernment, desperation can lead to deception. Predatory lenders prey on those with poor credit, offering quick cash with hidden fees, sky-high interest rates, and terms designed to trap rather than empower.

This chapter equips you with the wisdom to borrow strategically, avoid financial snares, and choose lenders that align with biblical principles of stewardship, fairness, and restoration.

Secured vs. Unsecured Loans – Choosing the Right Path

"Plans fail for lack of counsel, but with many advisers they succeed" (Proverbs 15:22).

Secured Loans require collateral—usually a savings deposit, vehicle, or other asset. Because the lender has something to fall back on, they offer:

- Lower interest rates
- Easier approval
- Longer repayment terms
- Credit-building potential

Unsecured Loans, on the other hand, are based solely on your creditworthiness. With poor credit, these often come with:

- Higher interest rates (20–36%+)
- Shorter terms (6–24 months)
- Smaller amounts ($500–$5,000)
- Stricter repayment schedules

Strategy: If you have any savings, choose a secured loan. You'll protect your credit, pay less in interest, and build trust with the lender. If unsecured is your only option, choose lenders with transparent terms and no prepayment penalties.

Best Lenders for Poor Credit Borrowers

"The Lord detests dishonest scales, but accurate weights find favor with Him" (Proverbs 11:1).

These lenders are known for working with consumers who have poor or limited credit, offering fair terms and credit-building opportunities:

1. Credit Unions (Apple FCU, Navy Federal, DCU)

- Offer credit builder loans and secured personal loans
- Report to all three bureaus
- Often waive fees for members
- Provide financial counseling

2. Self Financial

- Credit builder loans with no credit check
- Funds released after completion
- Reports monthly to all bureaus
- Ideal for thin or damaged credit files

3. Upgrade & Upstart

- Unsecured personal loans for credit scores as low as 580
- Fixed rates and terms
- Soft credit check for pre-approval
- Transparent fees

4. Avant & LendingPoint

- Specialize in subprime lending
- Fast funding and flexible terms
- Reports to bureaus
- Higher interest—use only if necessary

5. Local Community Banks

- Often offer secured loans with flexible underwriting
- Willing to consider income and stability over score
- May offer skip-a-pay or hardship options

These lenders operate with integrity and transparency—qualities that reflect Kingdom values in the financial realm.

How to Avoid Predatory Traps

"Be wise as serpents and harmless as doves" (Matthew 10:16).

Predatory lenders target vulnerable borrowers with flashy ads and fast approvals. But behind the scenes, they hide:

- Triple-digit APRs (100%+)
- Daily interest accrual
- Balloon payments
- Hidden fees and rollover traps

Red Flags:

- No credit check but instant approval
- No clear repayment schedule
- Pressure to sign immediately
- No physical address or customer service
- Promises of "guaranteed approval"

Protection Strategy:

- Always read the full loan agreement
- Use APR calculators to understand true cost
- Never borrow from payday or title loan companies
- Ask for written terms before signing
- Consult a financial counselor if unsure

"The prudent see danger and take refuge, but the simple keep going and pay the penalty" (Proverbs 27:12). Wisdom is your shield. Don't let urgency override discernment.

Final Word: Borrow with Purpose, Not Panic

Getting a loan with poor credit is possible—but it must be done with prayer, planning, and protection. The goal isn't just to get approved—it's to get empowered. Every loan should serve a purpose: rebuilding your credit, funding your calling, or bridging a temporary gap.

"Commit your works to the Lord, and your plans will be established" (Proverbs 16:3). Before you borrow, commit the decision to God. Ask for clarity. Seek wise counsel. And choose lenders who reflect His justice, mercy, and truth.

You're not just rebuilding your credit—you're rebuilding your confidence, your capacity, and your covenant with financial stewardship. Let every loan you take be a step toward legacy, not bondage.

***

Section 4: Experian Boost, UltraFICO, Rent Reporting, and More – Alternative Credit Strategies That Multiply Favor

When Traditional Credit Isn't Enough

"See, I am doing a new thing! Now it springs up; do you not perceive it?" (Isaiah 43:19).

For many consumers—especially those rebuilding or starting fresh—traditional credit scoring models don't tell the full story. You may pay your bills faithfully, manage your money wisely, and avoid debt traps, yet still be denied access to funding because your score lacks depth. That's where alternative credit strategies come in. These tools allow you to add positive data to your credit report that lenders can see and use to approve you for loans, cards, and housing.

Experian Boost, UltraFICO, and rent reporting are modern-day keys to unlock doors that were once closed. They reflect your real-life stewardship and give you credit for the faithfulness you've already shown.

Experian Boost – Turning Utility Bills into Credit Power

"Whoever is faithful with very little will also be faithful with much" (Luke 16:10).

Experian Boost allows you to add on-time payments for utilities, phone bills, and streaming services directly to your Experian credit report. It's free, fast, and can raise your score instantly—especially if you have a thin file.

How It Works:

- Connect your bank account securely
- Experian scans for eligible payments (Netflix, AT&T, water, etc.)
- Adds positive payment history to your report
- Updates your FICO Score 8 in real time

Why It Matters:

- Boosts score without taking on debt
- Helps qualify for credit cards and loans

- Reflects real-world financial discipline

This tool is grace in action—giving you credit for what you've already done faithfully.

UltraFICO – Your Bank Behavior Becomes Your Credit Strength

"The Lord sees not as man sees: man looks on the outward appearance, but the Lord looks on the heart" (1 Samuel 16:7).

UltraFICO goes deeper than traditional scoring. It evaluates your checking and savings account behavior—looking at how you manage money, not just how you borrow it. If you maintain a positive balance, avoid overdrafts, and save consistently, UltraFICO rewards you with a higher score.

Key Features:

- Uses banking data to supplement your FICO score
- Ideal for those with limited credit history
- Can raise score by 20–40 points
- Helps qualify for loans with better terms

Strategy:

- Keep $400+ in savings consistently
- Avoid overdrafts for 90+ days
- Use debit card responsibly

UltraFICO reflects the heart of stewardship—managing what you have with wisdom, even if it's not much.

Rent Reporting – Transforming Your Home into a Credit Asset

"By wisdom a house is built, and through understanding it is established" (Proverbs 24:3).

Rent reporting allows you to add your monthly rent payments to your credit report. If you've paid rent faithfully for years, this tool turns your roof into a resource. It's especially powerful for those who don't have mortgage history but want to show housing stability.

Top Rent Reporting Services:

- Esusu
- RentReporters
- Piñata
- CreditMyRent

Benefits:

- Adds tradeline with 12–24 months of history
- Boosts score for thin or rebuilding files
- Helps qualify for mortgages and apartment leases

Strategy:

- Choose a service that reports to all three bureaus
- Backdate payments if possible
- Ensure landlord verification is smooth

Rent reporting is a prophetic strategy—it redeems what was overlooked and turns it into favor.

Other Alternative Credit Tools to Explore

1. Kikoff

- Offers a $750 revolving tradeline for $5/month
- Reports to Equifax and Experian
- No hard inquiry or income check

2. Grow Credit

- Pays your subscriptions (Hulu, Disney+, etc.)
- Reports monthly to bureaus
- Free and paid plans available

3. Experian Go

- Helps new consumers build a credit profile
- Offers step-by-step guidance

- Connects to Boost and other tools

4. Utility Reporting via LevelCredit

- Adds electric, gas, and water payments
- Reports to TransUnion and Equifax
- Ideal for renters and low-income households

"The stone the builders rejected has become the cornerstone" (Psalm 118:22). These tools may seem small or unconventional, but they can become the cornerstone of your credit resurrection.

Final Word: Steward What You Already Have

You don't need a high income or perfect history to build credit—you need wisdom, consistency, and the right tools. Experian Boost, UltraFICO, rent reporting, and other alternatives allow you to turn everyday faithfulness into financial favor.

"Do not despise these small beginnings, for the Lord rejoices to see the work begin" (Zechariah 4:10). These tools are small beginnings. Use them with diligence, and watch your score rise, your access expand, and your testimony grow.

***

Section 5: How to Add Utility Bills, Subscriptions, and Insurance Payments to Your Credit File – Turning Everyday Faithfulness into Favor

Credit for What You're Already Doing

"Do not despise these small beginnings, for the Lord rejoices to see the work begin" (Zechariah 4:10).

Many people pay their bills faithfully every month—utilities, phone plans, streaming services, even insurance premiums—but never see those payments reflected in their credit score. Traditional credit models only reward debt management, not everyday stewardship. But now, new tools allow you to turn those routine payments into credit-building power. This chapter shows you how to add utility bills, subscriptions, and insurance payments to your credit file—legally, ethically, and strategically.

These aren't shortcuts. They're redemption strategies. They give you credit for the consistency you've already shown, and they reflect the biblical principle that faithfulness in small things leads to greater reward.

Utility Bills – Power, Water, and Gas as Credit Builders

"The wise store up knowledge, but the mouth of a fool invites ruin" (Proverbs 10:14).

Services like LevelCredit, eCredable, and Experian Boost allow you to report utility payments—including electricity, water, gas, and even trash collection—to the credit bureaus. These payments don't usually show up on your report unless you default. But with these tools, you can flip the script and use them to build credit instead.

How to Add Utility Payments:

1. Sign up with a reporting service (LevelCredit, eCredable Lift, or Experian Boost)
2. Link your bank account or utility provider
3. Verify payment history
4. Choose which bureaus to report to (some report to all three)

Benefits:

- Adds positive tradelines without debt
- Reflects real-world financial responsibility
- Can raise your score 10–40 points

This is stewardship in action—managing your household faithfully and letting that testimony speak.

Subscriptions – Streaming Services and Phone Plans as Credit Assets

"Whoever is faithful with very little will also be faithful with much" (Luke 16:10).

You may pay for Netflix, Hulu, Disney+, Spotify, or your cell phone every month. These payments show consistency, budgeting, and discipline. Experian Boost and Grow Credit allow you to report these subscriptions to the bureaus—turning entertainment into elevation.

How to Add Subscriptions:

- Use Grow Credit to pay subscriptions through a virtual card
- Link your bank account with Experian Boost to detect recurring payments
- Choose which subscriptions to include (Boost supports dozens)

Strategy:

- Keep subscriptions active and paid on time
- Use autopay to avoid missed payments
- Monitor your credit report monthly

These small payments become seeds—planted in faith, harvested in favor.

Insurance Payments – Protecting What You Have While Building What You Need

"The prudent see danger and take refuge, but the simple keep going and pay the penalty" (Proverbs 27:12).

Auto, renters, and life insurance premiums are often overlooked in credit building. But some platforms now allow you to report these payments—especially if paid through linked accounts or virtual cards.

How to Report Insurance Payments:

- Use eCredable Lift or Grow Credit if your insurance provider is supported
- Pay premiums through linked accounts
- Keep documentation of payment history

Why It Matters:

- Shows long-term financial commitment
- Adds depth to your credit profile
- Can help qualify for better rates and coverage

Insurance is protection—but now it can also be promotion.

Final Word: Steward What You Already Pay

You don't need new debt to build credit—you need new strategy. By reporting utility bills, subscriptions, and insurance payments, you turn everyday faithfulness into financial favor. These tools reward what God already sees: your consistency, your discipline, and your commitment to stewardship.

"The Lord will open the heavens, the storehouse of His bounty, to bless all the work of your hands" (Deuteronomy 28:12). Let your credit report reflect the work of your hands. Let every payment become a testimony. And let your score rise—not just because of what you borrow, but because of how you live.

You're not just building credit—you're building credibility, capacity, and covenant. Let every payment, every report, and every strategy reflect the restoration power of God in your financial life.

***

Section 6: DIY vs. Paid Services – Counting the Cost and Choosing Wisely

The Power of Stewardship in Credit Restoration

"Suppose one of you wants to build a tower. Won't you first sit down and estimate the cost to see if you have enough money to complete it?" (Luke 14:28).

When it comes to rebuilding credit, you'll face a critical decision early on: should you do it yourself (DIY), or pay for professional services? Both paths can lead to breakthrough, but they require different levels of time, money, and discernment. This chapter helps you weigh the cost, understand the risks, and choose the strategy that aligns with your season, your resources, and your calling.

Credit restoration is not just a financial process—it's a spiritual one. It requires wisdom, patience, and integrity. Whether you choose DIY or paid support, your goal is not just a higher score—it's a testimony of transformation.

DIY Credit Repair – Faithful Stewardship with Sweat Equity

"The plans of the diligent lead surely to abundance, but everyone who is hasty comes only to poverty" (Proverbs 21:5).

DIY credit repair means taking full responsibility for your restoration journey. You'll pull your own credit reports, dispute errors, negotiate with creditors, and build new tradelines—all without paying someone else to do it for you.

Benefits:

- No upfront cost
- Full control over every step
- Deeper understanding of your credit profile
- Empowers long-term financial literacy

Challenges:

- Time-consuming and detail-oriented
- Requires research and persistence

- Emotional toll when facing past mistakes
- No guarantees of success

DIY is for the diligent. It's for those who are ready to learn, grow, and fight for their financial future. It reflects the biblical principle of sowing in faith and reaping in wisdom.

Paid Services – Delegating with Discernment

"Plans fail for lack of counsel, but with many advisers they succeed" (Proverbs 15:22).

Paid credit repair services offer convenience and expertise. They handle disputes, monitor your credit, and sometimes offer tradeline access or legal support. But not all services are created equal—and some are outright predatory.

Benefits:

- Saves time and energy
- Access to professional tools and templates
- May include credit coaching or financial planning
- Can accelerate results if reputable

Risks:

- Monthly fees ($79–$149+)
- Long contracts with no guaranteed outcomes
- Some use illegal tactics (false disputes, credit sweeps)
- May discourage personal growth or understanding

Discernment Strategy:

- Check BBB ratings and reviews
- Ask for written service agreements
- Avoid companies that promise "guaranteed results"
- Never pay for services you don't understand

Paid services can be a blessing—but only if they operate in truth. *"The Lord detests dishonest scales, but accurate weights find favor with Him"*

(Proverbs 11:1). Choose companies that reflect Kingdom values of honesty, transparency, and empowerment.

When to Choose DIY vs. Paid Support

Choose DIY If:

- You have time and willingness to learn
- Your credit issues are minor or clear-cut
- You want to build long-term financial literacy
- You're on a tight budget

Choose Paid Services If:

- You're overwhelmed or emotionally triggered by your credit report
- You need legal help with collections or identity theft
- You're preparing for a major purchase (home, car) and need fast results
- You've vetted the company thoroughly

"There is a time for everything, and a season for every activity under the heavens" (Ecclesiastes 3:1). Your choice depends on your season. There's no shame in either path—only wisdom in choosing the one that bears fruit.

Final Word: Build with Integrity, Not Impulse

Whether you repair your credit yourself or hire help, the foundation must be integrity. Don't rush. Don't panic. Don't fall for flashy promises. Instead, commit your journey to God, seek wise counsel, and move forward with clarity.

"Commit your works to the Lord, and your plans will be established" (Proverbs 16:3). Your credit resurrection is not just about numbers—it's about stewardship, testimony, and transformation. DIY or paid, let every step reflect the wisdom, grace, and favor of Heaven.

Part III: Access Hidden Assets – Unlocking What's Already Yours

The Kingdom Principle of Hidden Provision

"I will give you the treasures of darkness and hidden riches of secret places, that you may know that I, the Lord, who call you by your name, am the God of Israel" (Isaiah 45:3).

In the natural, hidden assets are overlooked resources—money, credit, or opportunities that exist but aren't easily seen. In the spiritual, hidden assets are divine provisions waiting to be revealed through obedience, wisdom, and revelation. Part III is about uncovering what's already yours: financial tools, reporting strategies, and overlooked accounts that can accelerate your credit resurrection and unlock access to funding, favor, and freedom.

This isn't about chasing what's flashy—it's about stewarding what's buried. God often hides provision in places that require faith to find. Your breakthrough may not come from new income, but from recognizing and activating what's already in your possession.

Hidden Tradelines – Accounts You Didn't Know Could Build Credit

"The stone the builders rejected has become the cornerstone" (Psalm 118:22).

Many consumers overlook tradelines that already exist in their financial life. These include:

- Rent payments
- Utility bills
- Streaming subscriptions
- Insurance premiums
- Cell phone plans

With tools like Experian Boost, UltraFICO, LevelCredit, and Grow Credit, you can report these payments to the credit bureaus and turn overlooked obligations into credit-building assets. These aren't new debts—they're existing responsibilities that now work in your favor.

Strategy:

- Link your bank account to Boost or UltraFICO
- Use virtual cards to pay subscriptions through Grow Credit
- Report rent through Esusu or RentReporters
- Backdate payments for maximum impact

These hidden tradelines reflect your faithfulness. You've already paid—now it's time to be rewarded.

Business Credit Assets – Building a Second Credit Profile

"Enlarge the place of your tent, stretch your tent curtains wide, do not hold back" (Isaiah 54:2).

Forming an LLC and opening a business checking account allows you to build a second credit profile—separate from your personal score. Even without revenue, you can access:

- Business secured credit cards
- Net-30 vendor accounts
- Toll-free business phone lines that report
- EIN-based funding opportunities

These assets are hidden in structure. The moment you establish your business identity, banks begin to treat you differently. You gain access to funding, partnerships, and credibility that were previously unavailable.

Strategy:

- Form an LLC and get an EIN
- Open a business checking account
- Apply for business credit cards with personal guarantee
- Use vendor accounts to build payment history

Your business is not just a dream—it's a doorway. Hidden assets await those who build with intention.

Dormant Accounts – Reviving What Was Forgotten

"Can these dry bones live?" (Ezekiel 37:3).

Old accounts—closed, inactive, or forgotten—can still carry weight. If you had a credit card or loan with perfect history that was closed, you may be able to:

- Request reinstatement
- Reopen the account
- Use the history to qualify for new credit

Even closed accounts with positive history remain on your report for up to 10 years. They contribute to your average age and payment history—two of the most powerful score factors.

Strategy:

- Review your full credit report for dormant accounts
- Contact lenders to request reopening or product change
- Use the history to support new applications

God specializes in resurrection. What you thought was dead may still carry life.

Final Word: Seek and You Shall Find

Hidden assets are not hidden to punish you—they're hidden to prepare you. They require diligence, prayer, and revelation to uncover. But once activated, they multiply your momentum and accelerate your breakthrough.

"Ask, and it will be given to you; seek, and you will find; knock, and the door will be opened to you" (Matthew 7:7).

Part III is your invitation to seek. To dig. To activate. You're not starting from scratch—you're starting from strength. Let every hidden asset become a revealed testimony. Let every overlooked resource become a tool of restoration. And let your credit journey reflect the glory of a God who hides treasures in secret places—just for you.

***

Chapter 7: Buying Cars & Homes from Government Auctions – Redeeming Value Others Overlook

Divine Deals in Unlikely Places

"The stone the builders rejected has become the cornerstone" (Psalm 118:22).

Government auctions are one of the most overlooked financial strategies for acquiring high-value assets—vehicles, homes, land, and equipment—at a fraction of their market price. These auctions are often the result of repossessions, forfeitures, or surplus inventory, and while the world may see them as discarded or undesirable, the wise see opportunity. Just as God redeems what others reject, these auctions allow you to redeem value others have missed.

This chapter reveals how to navigate government auctions with discernment, strategy, and biblical stewardship—turning overlooked assets into tools for transportation, housing, and generational wealth.

What Are Government Auctions?

"I will give you the treasures of darkness and hidden riches of secret places..." (Isaiah 45:3).

Government auctions are public sales hosted by federal, state, or local agencies to liquidate seized, repossessed, or surplus property. These include:

- Vehicles from law enforcement or IRS seizures
- Homes from HUD, VA, or tax foreclosure
- Land from county surplus
- Equipment from military or municipal departments

These assets are often sold below market value, with minimal competition and transparent bidding processes. The key is knowing where to look and how to prepare.

Buying Cars – Reliable Transportation at a Redeemed Price

"The steps of a good man are ordered by the Lord..." (Psalm 37:23).

Cars sold at government auctions often come from fleet programs, police departments, or IRS seizures. They're well-maintained, low-mileage, and priced to move.

Where to Buy:

- GovDeals.com
- GSA Auctions (General Services Administration)
- Local sheriff or county auctions
- PublicSurplus.com

Strategy:

- Research vehicle history (VIN reports)
- Attend preview days to inspect condition
- Set a firm budget and avoid emotional bidding
- Factor in registration, repairs, and transport

Buying a car this way is not just frugal—it's prophetic. You're reclaiming what was surrendered and using it to move forward.

Buying Homes – Restoring What Was Lost

"They will rebuild the ancient ruins and restore the places long devastated..." (Isaiah 61:4).

Government home auctions include properties from HUD, VA, USDA, and tax foreclosure sales. These homes may need repairs, but they offer a chance to own property at 30–70% below market value.

Where to Buy:

- HUDHomestore.com
- Treasury.gov auctions
- County tax deed sales
- Auction.com

Strategy:

- Get pre-approved for financing or prepare cash
- Attend local tax deed sales in person

- Research liens, title status, and occupancy
- Budget for renovation and legal fees

These homes are more than buildings—they're redemption stories. You're restoring what was lost and reclaiming territory for your family and future.

Risks and Rewards – Wisdom Before Wealth

"The prudent see danger and take refuge, but the simple keep going and pay the penalty" (Proverbs 27:12).

Government auctions offer incredible value, but they require wisdom:

- Assets are sold "as-is" with no warranties
- Some properties may have hidden liens or damage
- Bidding can be competitive and fast-paced
- You must act quickly but not impulsively

Protection Strategy:

- Always inspect before bidding
- Use escrow or title services for real estate
- Avoid auctions that lack transparency
- Pray before you purchase—ask for peace and clarity

This is not gambling—it's guided stewardship. You're not chasing deals; you're walking in divine direction.

Final Word: Reclaiming What Others Discarded

Government auctions are a prophetic picture of restoration. What others gave up, you can redeem. What was seized, you can steward. What was forgotten, you can revive.

"He raises the poor from the dust and lifts the needy from the ash heap; He seats them with princes..." (Psalm 113:7–8).

Buying cars and homes from government auctions isn't just financial strategy—it's Kingdom strategy. It reflects God's heart to restore, rebuild, and reposition His people. Let every bid be a step of faith. Let every purchase be a testimony. And let your journey reflect the God who turns ashes into beauty and auctions into abundance.

***

Section 1: Redeemed Property – Buying Cars and Homes Through GSA, Treasury, IRS, and U.S. Marshals Auctions

God's Provision Through Unlikely Channels

"The earth is the Lord's, and everything in it, the world, and all who live in it" (Psalm 24:1).

God's provision doesn't always come through traditional means. Sometimes, He opens doors through systems the world overlooks—government auctions included. These auctions are modern-day examples of divine strategy, where assets once seized, forfeited, or abandoned are made available at a fraction of their value. For the wise and prepared, these are opportunities to acquire cars, homes, and land that can serve as tools for transportation, housing, or investment.

This chapter explores how to access these hidden treasures through federal auction platforms like GSA, Treasury, IRS, and U.S. Marshals Service, and whether it's possible to purchase abandoned or towed vehicles. With prayer, research, and stewardship, you can turn what others discarded into a blessing for your household.

GSA Auctions – Government Surplus at Your Fingertips

"The wealth of the sinner is stored up for the righteous" (Proverbs 13:22).

The General Services Administration (GSA) manages surplus federal property, including thousands of vehicles and real estate assets. These are often well-maintained government fleet vehicles—sedans, trucks, SUVs, and even specialty equipment—sold at public auction.

How to Access:

- Visit gsaauctions.gov
- Create a free account
- Browse listings by state, category, or asset type
- Bid online and arrange pickup or closing

Why It Matters:

- Vehicles are often low-mileage and regularly serviced
- Homes and land may be undervalued
- Transparent bidding process

GSA auctions are a practical way to access quality assets without predatory pricing. It's a reminder that God can use even bureaucratic systems to bless His people.

Treasury and IRS Auctions – Reclaiming What Was Forfeited

"I will restore to you the years that the swarming locust has eaten..." (Joel 2:25).

The U.S. Department of the Treasury and the IRS conduct auctions of seized property—homes, vehicles, jewelry, and business assets—often taken due to unpaid taxes or criminal activity. These assets are sold to the public to recover owed funds, but they also represent redemption opportunities for buyers.

Where to Start:

- Treasury Auctions
- IRS Real and Personal Property Sales

What You'll Find:

- Residential and commercial properties
- Luxury and economy vehicles
- Business equipment and collectibles

Strategy:

- Research property thoroughly (title, liens, condition)
- Attend in-person or online auctions
- Secure financing or prepare cash in advance

These auctions are not just financial—they're prophetic. You're reclaiming what was lost and restoring it for Kingdom use.

U.S. Marshals Auctions – High-Value Assets with High Potential

"He raises the poor from the dust and lifts the needy from the ash heap; He seats them with princes..." (Psalm 113:7–8).

The U.S. Marshals Service auctions off assets seized in federal criminal cases—luxury cars, real estate, boats, and more. These auctions often include high-end items at deeply discounted prices.

How to Participate:

- Visit usmarshals.gov and follow links to asset forfeiture auctions
- Auctions are managed by contracted vendors (e.g., Apple Auctioneering, CWS Marketing)
- Register and bid online or in person

Why It's Strategic:

- Assets are often in excellent condition
- Less competition than traditional markets
- Can be used for personal use, resale, or ministry

These are modern-day "spoils of war"—resources once used for unrighteous purposes, now available for righteous stewardship.

Can You Buy Abandoned or Towed Cars?

"I will give you hidden treasures, riches stored in secret places..." (Isaiah 45:3).

Yes, in many cities and counties, abandoned or towed vehicles are auctioned to the public. These auctions are typically managed by local police departments, towing companies, or municipal surplus divisions.

How to Find Them:

- Search "[Your City] police impound auction" or "[County] towed vehicle auction"
- Check with local towing companies or city surplus departments
- Look for listings on PublicSurplus.com or GovDeals.com

What to Expect:

- Vehicles sold "as-is" with no warranty

- Some may need repairs or title work
- Bidding is often in person or through local auctioneers

Tips:

- Inspect vehicles before bidding
- Bring cash or certified funds
- Verify title status and registration process

These vehicles may look forgotten, but they carry potential. Like David choosing five smooth stones, you may find your next vehicle in an unlikely place—ready to serve your purpose.

Final Word: Redeem, Restore, Rebuild

Government auctions are not just about getting a deal—they're about redeeming what others have abandoned. Whether it's a car, a home, or a piece of land, these assets can become part of your testimony. They reflect God's ability to restore what was lost, to provide through unexpected channels, and to bless His people with wisdom and favor.

"The meek shall inherit the land and delight themselves in abundant peace" (Psalm 37:11).

Approach these opportunities with prayer, preparation, and purpose. Let every bid be guided by discernment. Let every purchase be a step toward legacy. And let your journey reflect the God who turns forfeiture into favor and auctions into abundance.

***

Section 2: How to Bid, Inspect, and Win Seized Assets – Stewarding Opportunity with Strategy and Faith

The Blessing Hidden in Seizure

"I will give you the treasures of darkness and hidden riches of secret places..." (Isaiah 45:3).

Seized assets—whether vehicles, homes, land, or equipment—are often the result of forfeiture, tax delinquency, or criminal investigations. While the world may see these items as tainted or undesirable, God sees them as redeemable. These assets, once lost or abandoned, can become tools of restoration for those who walk in wisdom and stewardship. Bidding on seized assets is not just about getting a deal—it's about reclaiming what was surrendered and using it for Kingdom purpose.

This chapter equips you with practical steps to bid, inspect, and win seized assets legally and ethically, while also exploring how mobile homes can be purchased through the NACA program as a side strategy for affordable housing.

Step 1: How to Bid – Entering the Marketplace with Discernment

"Commit your works to the Lord, and your plans will be established" (Proverbs 16:3).

Government auctions are typically hosted online or in person through agencies like the IRS, U.S. Marshals Service, Treasury Department, and local municipalities. To bid successfully, you must first register, understand the terms, and set a budget.

Bidding Strategy:

- Create accounts on platforms like GovDeals, GSA Auctions, Treasury Auctions, and CWS Marketing
- Research the asset's estimated value and condition
- Set a maximum bid and stick to it—avoid emotional bidding
- Monitor auction timelines and place bids strategically (often near closing)

Bidding is a form of spiritual discipline. It requires patience, restraint, and clarity. You're not just buying—you're building.

Step 2: How to Inspect – Seeing Beyond the Surface

"The prudent see danger and take refuge, but the simple keep going and pay the penalty" (Proverbs 27:12).

Most seized assets are sold "as-is," which means inspection is critical. Whether it's a car, home, or mobile unit, you must assess its condition before bidding.

Inspection Tips:

- Attend preview days or request inspection appointments
- Bring a mechanic or contractor if possible
- Review photos, VIN reports, and property disclosures
- Ask questions about title status, liens, and repairs

Inspection is about wisdom. It's the difference between a blessing and a burden. Don't skip this step—God honors preparation.

Step 3: How to Win – Closing the Deal with Integrity

"Let your yes be yes, and your no be no..." (Matthew 5:37).

Winning a bid is only the beginning. You must follow through with payment, paperwork, and pickup or closing. Each agency has its own rules, but the principles remain the same.

Winning Strategy:

- Pay promptly using certified funds or approved methods
- Complete all required documentation (title transfer, deed recording)
- Arrange transport or occupancy
- Keep records for tax and legal purposes

Winning is not just about acquisition—it's about stewardship. You're taking possession of something that was once lost and restoring it to purpose.

Side Note: Buying Mobile Homes Through the NACA Program

"They will build houses and dwell in them; they will plant vineyards and eat their fruit" (Isaiah 65:21).

The Neighborhood Assistance Corporation of America (NACA) is a nonprofit organization offering affordable homeownership solutions. While traditionally focused on single-family homes, NACA has expanded its reach to include mobile and manufactured homes in certain regions.

How It Works:

- Attend a NACA Homebuyer Workshop to begin the process
- Complete financial counseling and qualification steps
- Work with a NACA-approved realtor or builder to locate mobile home options
- Secure financing with no down payment, no closing costs, and below-market interest rates

Why It Matters:

- Mobile homes offer affordable entry into homeownership
- NACA's mission aligns with biblical justice—empowering the underserved
- You can own land and home without predatory lending

This is a modern-day fulfillment of Isaiah's promise—building and dwelling in homes that reflect dignity, stability, and legacy.

Final Word: Redeem What Was Lost, Rebuild What Was Broken

Seized assets and mobile homes may not look glamorous, but they carry hidden value. With prayer, preparation, and strategy, you can turn these opportunities into vehicles of restoration. You're not just acquiring property—you're reclaiming territory.

"The meek shall inherit the land and delight themselves in abundant peace" (Psalm 37:11).

Bid with wisdom. Inspect with discernment. Win with integrity. And let every asset you acquire reflect the goodness of a God who redeems, restores, and rebuilds through the hands of His people.

***

Yes, real-life examples of $1 homes and $500 vehicles exist—especially through government auctions and surplus sales. These opportunities reflect biblical principles of redemption, stewardship, and restoration.

Section 3: Real-Life Examples of $1 Homes and $500 Vehicles – Redeeming What Others Overlook

The God of Unlikely Provision

"The stone the builders rejected has become the cornerstone" (Psalm 118:22).

In the world's economy, value is often measured by appearance, prestige, or popularity. But in the Kingdom, value is found in redemption. Just as God restores what others discard, government auctions and surplus programs offer real-life opportunities to acquire homes and vehicles for pennies on the dollar. These aren't gimmicks—they're testimonies of favor, strategy, and divine timing.

From $1 homes in distressed neighborhoods to $500 vehicles from police impounds, these examples prove that breakthrough doesn't always come through abundance—it often comes through wisdom.

$1 Homes – Restoring Communities and Building Legacy

"They will rebuild the ancient ruins and restore the places long devastated..." (Isaiah 61:4).

Cities like Detroit, Buffalo, and Gary have offered homes for as little as $1 through land bank programs and revitalization initiatives. These properties are often abandoned or tax-foreclosed, but they come with the opportunity to rebuild, restore, and reclaim territory.

Real-Life Example:

- *Bid4Assets.com* regularly lists $1 homes in counties across the U.S., including Pennsylvania, Michigan, and Indiana.
- Buyers must commit to renovating the property and living in it or using it for community development.
- Some programs require proof of income or renovation plans, but the entry cost is minimal.

These homes are more than structures—they're seeds of restoration. What others left behind, you can revive.

$500 Vehicles – Reliable Transportation at a Redeemed Price

"He raises the poor from the dust and lifts the needy from the ash heap; He seats them with princes..." (Psalm 113:7–8).

Government vehicle auctions—hosted by police departments, federal agencies, and municipalities—often include cars, trucks, and SUVs starting at $500 or less. These vehicles may be seized, repossessed, or retired from fleet service, but many are in excellent condition.

Real-Life Example:

- *Gov-Sources.org* reports vehicles like a 2015 BMW 335i sold for $16,900 (book value $40,250), and a 2016 Nissan Altima for $14,350 (book value $22,000).
- Local impound auctions have sold older sedans and pickups for $500–$1,000, especially in cities like Atlanta, Houston, and Chicago.
- Buyers often find vehicles with clean titles, service records, and low mileage.

These vehicles are modern-day "spoils of war"—repossessed, repurposed, and ready to serve a new mission.

Stewardship Over Status

"Better a little with righteousness than much gain with injustice" (Proverbs 16:8).

Buying a $1 home or a $500 vehicle isn't about being cheap—it's about being strategic. It's about seeing value where others see waste. It's about walking in wisdom, not impulse. These opportunities require research, patience, and sometimes renovation—but they reflect the heart of God: to restore, rebuild, and redeem.

Keys to Success:

- Research auction platforms and local surplus programs
- Inspect assets before bidding
- Budget for repairs and legal fees
- Pray for discernment and divine timing

Final Word: Redeem What Was Rejected

"I will give you hidden treasures, riches stored in secret places..." (Isaiah 45:3).

Real-life examples of $1 homes and $500 vehicles prove that God's provision often comes through unexpected channels. These assets may look forgotten, but they carry purpose. With faith, strategy, and stewardship, you can turn these opportunities into testimonies of breakthrough.

Let your purchase reflect your purpose. Let your restoration reflect His redemption. And let your journey prove that favor isn't always expensive—it's often hidden in plain sight.

Sources: Bid4Assets $1 Home Auctions Gov-Sources Repossessed Vehicle Auctions.

***

Section 4: The USDA Land Purchasing Grant – Reclaiming Territory Through Faith and Federal Favor

God's Promise to Possess the Land

"Every place that the sole of your foot will tread upon I have given to you, as I said to Moses" (Joshua 1:3).

In the natural, land ownership is a symbol of stability, legacy, and opportunity. In the spiritual, it represents inheritance, dominion, and covenant. The USDA's land purchasing programs—especially those targeting underserved communities—are modern-day manifestations of this promise. Through grants, loans, and cooperative agreements, the USDA is helping individuals and families reclaim land that can be used for farming, housing, and generational impact.

This chapter explores how to access these resources, steward them wisely, and walk in the authority God has already given to possess the land.

USDA Farm Ownership Loans – Financing the Promise

"The Lord will open the heavens, the storehouse of His bounty, to bless all the work of your hands" (Deuteronomy 28:12).

The USDA's Farm Service Agency (FSA) offers **Direct Farm Ownership Loans** to help eligible applicants purchase farmland, construct buildings, and make long-term improvements. These loans are designed for those who cannot obtain credit elsewhere, including beginning farmers, veterans, and socially disadvantaged individuals.

Key Features:

- Up to $600,000 in funding
- Low interest rates
- No down payment required in some cases
- 40-year repayment terms

Eligibility:

- Must demonstrate farming experience or intent

- Must meet income and credit guidelines
- Must use land for agricultural purposes

This is more than financing—it's favor. It's a way to turn vision into vineyard, and calling into cultivation.

Increasing Land Access Program – Grants for Underserved Producers

"They will build houses and dwell in them; they will plant vineyards and eat their fruit" (Isaiah 65:21).

Launched under the American Rescue Plan and expanded through the Inflation Reduction Act, the **Increasing Land Access Program** provides grants to nonprofits, cooperatives, and tribal entities that help underserved producers acquire land and build agricultural enterprises.

Program Goals:

- Increase land ownership among minority and underserved farmers
- Support heirs' property resolution and land succession
- Provide technical assistance and business planning
- Expand access to capital and markets

In 2023, the USDA awarded **$300 million across 50 projects** in 40 states and territories. These grants don't go directly to individuals, but through trusted organizations that walk alongside applicants to help them succeed.

How to Access:

- Connect with local USDA offices or nonprofit partners
- Ask about land access grants and cooperative agreements
- Attend workshops and training sessions
- Prepare documentation and business plans

This is a divine strategy—God using institutions to restore what was lost and empower what was overlooked.

Stewardship and Strategy

"By wisdom a house is built, and through understanding it is established" (Proverbs 24:3).

Land ownership is not just about possession—it's about stewardship. Whether you receive a loan or benefit from a grant, you must manage the land with integrity, diligence, and vision. This includes:

- Creating a sustainable farming plan
- Maintaining the property
- Using the land to bless others
- Documenting progress and honoring agreements

God doesn't just give land—He gives instruction. Your success will come not just from access, but from obedience.

Final Word: Possess the Land with Purpose

"You will inherit a double portion in your land, and everlasting joy will be yours" (Isaiah 61:7).

The USDA land purchasing programs are more than policy—they're prophetic. They reflect God's heart to restore territory, empower families, and build legacy. Whether through loans or grants, you have access to tools that can turn your dreams into deeds.

Step forward. Apply boldly. Steward faithfully. And let your land ownership journey reflect the goodness of a God who gives seed to the sower and land to the faithful.

Sources: USDA Grants and Loans Overview Increasing Land Access Program Details

***

Section 5: Securing the Inheritance – Legal Precision for Lasting Legacy

Protecting the Promise with Precision

"Let all things be done decently and in order" (1 Corinthians 14:40).

When it comes to passing down property and preserving generational wealth, spiritual intention must be matched with legal precision. Many families lose homes, land, or assets not because of a lack of love—but because of a lack of clarity. God is a God of order, and when we align our legal documents with that order, we protect the inheritance He's entrusted to us. This chapter unpacks the critical steps to ensure your home is properly titled, insured, and positioned for generational transfer—without unnecessary taxes, disputes, or delays.

Match the Names on the Title Exactly

"A good name is more desirable than great riches; to be esteemed is better than silver or gold" (Proverbs 22:1).

When transferring or protecting property, the names on the deed must match exactly with the names on the title. This means:

- No nicknames or abbreviations
- No missing middle initials or suffixes
- No adding or removing names without legal documentation

Even a small discrepancy can delay or derail a transfer, especially during probate or trust administration. This is about integrity and accuracy—ensuring that what God has given is not lost due to oversight.

File the Deed with the County

"Write the vision and make it plain on tablets, that he may run who reads it" (Habakkuk 2:2).

It's not enough to sign a deed—you must file it with the county recorder's office. Until it's recorded, the transfer is not legally recognized. This step:

- Establishes public record of ownership

- Protects against future disputes or fraud
- Ensures the property is legally tied to the trust or individual

Unfiled deeds are like unspoken promises—they carry no legal weight. Filing the deed is a prophetic act of sealing what God has given you.

Add the Trust as an Additional Insured

"The prudent see danger and take refuge..." (Proverbs 27:12).

If your home is held in a trust, the trust must be listed as an additional insured on your homeowner's insurance policy. This ensures:

- The trust is covered in case of damage or liability
- Claims are not denied due to a mismatch in ownership
- The property remains protected under the correct legal entity

This is about covering your house in both the natural and the spiritual. Just as we plead the blood of Jesus over our homes, we must also ensure our legal documents reflect the true ownership structure.

Make Your Children Successor Beneficiaries—Not Current Owners

"An inheritance claimed too soon will not be blessed at the end" (Proverbs 20:21).

It may seem loving to add your children as current owners of your home, but doing so can create unintended consequences:

- They become legal co-owners immediately
- The home becomes subject to their debts, divorces, or legal issues
- You may lose control over refinancing, selling, or managing the property

Instead, name your children as *successor beneficiaries* in your trust. This means:

- They inherit the home only after your passing
- The property avoids probate
- You retain full control during your lifetime

This honors the biblical principle of timing—blessing your children without burdening them or jeopardizing your own stability.

Final Word: Build Legacy with Legal Wisdom

"Through wisdom a house is built, and by understanding it is established; by knowledge the rooms are filled with all precious and pleasant riches" (Proverbs 24:3–4).

God has called you to build legacy, not just wealth. That legacy must be protected with wisdom, documented with clarity, and passed down with order. Matching names, filing deeds, insuring trusts, and structuring inheritance properly are not just legal tasks—they are acts of stewardship.

Don't let confusion rob your children of their inheritance. Secure the promise. Protect the house. And let your legacy be a testimony of both spiritual faithfulness and legal wisdom.

***

Chapter 8: How to Buy a House with Poor Credit or No Credit – Faith-Fueled Homeownership Strategies

God's Promise of Dwelling and Dominion

"They will build houses and dwell in them; they will plant vineyards and eat their fruit" (Isaiah 65:21).

Homeownership is more than a financial milestone—it's a prophetic act of stability, legacy, and dominion. Yet for many, poor credit or no credit feels like a locked door. The good news is that God specializes in opening doors no man can shut (Revelation 3:8), and there are practical, proven strategies to help you buy a home even when your credit history is limited or damaged.

This chapter reveals how to navigate the housing market with faith and wisdom, using alternative financing, government programs, and creative solutions to step into the promise of homeownership.

Step 1: Know Your Credit Reality and Prepare in Faith

"My people are destroyed for lack of knowledge..." (Hosea 4:6).

Before you begin, pull your credit reports from all three bureaus (Experian, Equifax, TransUnion). Understand what lenders see and identify any errors or outdated information. Even if your score is low, knowing your position allows you to plan strategically.

Action Steps:

- Dispute inaccuracies
- Pay down small debts
- Add positive tradelines (secured cards, rent reporting)
- Document consistent income and savings

Faith doesn't ignore facts—it prepares to overcome them. Your credit score is not your destiny; it's a starting point.

Step 2: Explore Government and Nonprofit Programs

"The Lord will open the heavens, the storehouse of His bounty, to bless all the work of your hands..." (Deuteronomy 28:12).

Several programs exist to help buyers with poor or no credit purchase homes. These include:

FHA Loans

- Backed by the Federal Housing Administration
- Accept scores as low as 580 (or 500 with larger down payment)
- Require 3.5% down and steady income

USDA Loans

- For rural and suburban areas
- No down payment required
- Flexible credit guidelines

VA Loans

- For veterans and active-duty service members
- No down payment, no PMI, and lenient credit requirements

NACA (Neighborhood Assistance Corporation of America)

- No credit score requirement
- No down payment, closing costs, or fees
- Requires financial counseling and community involvement

These programs reflect God's heart for justice—making housing accessible to those who've been overlooked.

Step 3: Use Alternative Credit and Manual Underwriting

"The Lord does not look at the things people look at. People look at the outward appearance, but the Lord looks at the heart" (1 Samuel 16:7).

If you don't have traditional credit, lenders can use alternative data to evaluate your reliability. This includes:

- Rent payments
- Utility bills
- Insurance premiums

- Cell phone and subscription payments

Some lenders offer **manual underwriting**, where they assess your financial behavior instead of relying solely on your score. This is ideal for those with consistent income but no credit history.

Strategy:

- Keep detailed records of payments
- Use Experian Boost or rent reporting tools
- Work with credit unions or community banks

This approach mirrors God's justice—looking beyond the surface to see the truth of your stewardship.

Step 4: Consider Lease-to-Own and Owner Financing

"You will live in houses you did not build..." (Deuteronomy 6:11).

Creative financing options allow you to bypass traditional lenders:

- **Lease-to-own** agreements let you rent while building equity
- **Owner financing** allows the seller to act as the lender, often with flexible terms
- **Land contracts** offer gradual ownership with monthly payments

These options require discernment and legal review, but they can be powerful tools for those rebuilding credit.

God can use unconventional paths to fulfill conventional promises. Don't limit His provision to one method.

Final Word: Homeownership Is a Covenant, Not Just a Contract

"By wisdom a house is built, and through understanding it is established" (Proverbs 24:3).

Buying a home with poor or no credit is possible—but it requires faith, strategy, and stewardship. You're not just purchasing property—you're stepping into a covenant of stability, legacy, and dominion. Whether through FHA, USDA, NACA, or creative financing, God has made a way for you to dwell in the land.

Prepare your heart. Strengthen your hands. And walk boldly toward the promise. Your home is not just a structure—it's a testimony of restoration.

***

Section 1: FHA, USDA, and Down Payment Assistance Programs – Unlocking Homeownership Through Faith and Favor

God's Heart for Housing and Stability

"My people will live in peaceful dwelling places, in secure homes, in undisturbed places of rest" (Isaiah 32:18).

Homeownership is more than a financial goal—it's a prophetic symbol of stability, inheritance, and divine provision. Yet for many, the barriers of poor credit, limited income, or lack of savings feel insurmountable. Thankfully, there are programs designed to bridge that gap. FHA loans, USDA loans, and down payment assistance programs are modern-day tools of favor—created to help everyday people step into the promise of homeownership.

This chapter explores how these programs work, who qualifies, and how to use them with wisdom and faith to secure your home and build legacy.

FHA Loans – Grace for the Rebuilder

"Though your beginning was small, your latter days will be very great" (Job 8:7).

The Federal Housing Administration (FHA) offers loans specifically designed for buyers with low credit scores or limited savings. These loans are backed by the government, making lenders more willing to approve applicants who might otherwise be denied.

Key Features:

- Credit scores as low as 580 (or 500 with 10% down)
- Down payments as low as 3.5%
- Flexible income and debt requirements
- Allows gift funds for down payment

Why It Matters:

- Ideal for first-time buyers or those rebuilding after financial hardship

- Can be paired with down payment assistance programs
- Reflects grace in the lending system—favor for those starting over

FHA loans are a picture of redemption. They don't require perfection—just progress.

USDA Loans – Possessing the Land with No Down Payment

"Every place that the sole of your foot will tread upon I have given to you..." (Joshua 1:3).

The U.S. Department of Agriculture (USDA) offers home loans for properties in rural and suburban areas. These loans are designed to promote homeownership in underserved regions and come with generous terms.

Key Features:

- No down payment required
- Low fixed interest rates
- Flexible credit guidelines
- Must be in a USDA-eligible area

Eligibility:

- Income must fall within area limits
- Property must be primary residence
- Must meet basic credit and income standards

USDA loans reflect God's promise to give land to His people. They open doors to territory that others overlook.

Down Payment Assistance – Help for the Faithful

"The Lord will open the heavens, the storehouse of His bounty, to bless all the work of your hands" (Deuteronomy 28:12).

Down payment assistance (DPA) programs provide grants, forgivable loans, or deferred-payment loans to help cover the upfront costs of buying a home. These programs are offered by states, cities, nonprofits, and even some lenders.

Types of Assistance:

- Grants (no repayment required)
- Forgivable loans (repaid only if you sell early)
- Deferred loans (paid later or at sale)
- Matched savings programs

Who Qualifies:

- First-time homebuyers
- Low-to-moderate income families
- Veterans, teachers, and public servants
- Those completing homebuyer education courses

DPA programs are a reflection of divine provision—help in the time of need, and favor for those who've been faithful.

Final Word: Step Into the Promise

"You will inherit a double portion in your land, and everlasting joy will be yours" (Isaiah 61:7).

FHA, USDA, and down payment assistance programs are not just financial tools—they're keys to prophetic fulfillment. They allow you to possess land, build legacy, and dwell in peace. Whether you're rebuilding credit, starting fresh, or stepping out in faith, these programs are designed to support your journey.

Don't let fear or lack stop you. Prepare your documents. Attend workshops. Ask questions. And move forward with confidence. Your home is not just a purchase—it's a promise. And God has already made provision for you to walk in it.

***

Section 2: The Truth About 0% Interest and Creative Financing – Discernment in the Deal

Not Every Offer Is a Blessing

"The simple believe anything, but the prudent give thought to their steps" (Proverbs 14:15).

In the world of credit and financing, flashy offers like "0% interest" can seem like divine favor. But not every deal is a blessing. Some financial institutions use promotional rates to lure consumers into agreements that carry hidden risks. One common trap is the retroactive interest clause—where missed payments or early termination trigger a chargeback of all the interest that was previously waived. What looked like a season of grace can quickly become a burden of debt.

This chapter equips you to discern the fine print, understand the spiritual principle of stewardship, and explore creative financing options like lease-to-own and seller financing with wisdom and integrity.

The 0% Interest Trap – When Grace Turns into a Bill

"Be sure you know the condition of your flocks, give careful attention to your herds" (Proverbs 27:23).

Many credit cards and loans offer 0% interest for a limited time—often 6 to 18 months. While this can be a powerful tool for debt consolidation or large purchases, it comes with conditions. If you miss a payment, exceed your limit, or fail to pay off the balance before the promotional period ends, the lender may retroactively apply interest to the entire balance from day one.

What to Watch For:

- Deferred interest vs. waived interest (deferred means it can come back)
- Penalty APRs for missed payments
- Retroactive interest clauses in the fine print
- Balance transfer fees and hidden costs

Strategy:

- Set automatic payments to avoid late fees
- Pay off the balance before the promo ends
- Read the full agreement before signing

This is a spiritual lesson in stewardship. Just as God calls us to count the cost before building (Luke 14:28), we must count the cost before borrowing—even when the rate looks like a miracle.

Lease-to-Own – Renting with a Path to Ownership

"You will live in houses you did not build..." (Deuteronomy 6:11).

Lease-to-own agreements allow you to rent a home with the option to buy it later. A portion of your monthly rent may be credited toward the purchase price, and you lock in the price upfront. This is ideal for buyers with poor credit or limited savings who need time to qualify for a mortgage.

Benefits:

- Immediate occupancy
- Builds equity while renting
- Fixed purchase price
- Time to improve credit or save

Risks:

- Non-refundable option fees
- Loss of equity if you don't buy
- Responsibility for repairs and taxes

Discernment Strategy:

- Get the agreement in writing
- Work with a real estate attorney
- Ensure the seller owns the property free and clear

Lease-to-own is a prophetic picture of transition—renting in faith while preparing to possess the promise.

Seller Financing – When the Owner Becomes the Lender

"The wealth of the wicked is stored up for the righteous" (Proverbs 13:22).

Seller financing allows the homeowner to act as the bank. Instead of applying for a traditional mortgage, you make payments directly to the seller—often with flexible terms and minimal credit requirements.

Benefits:

- No bank approval needed
- Customizable down payment and interest rate
- Faster closing process
- Ideal for buyers with unique financial situations

Risks:

- Higher interest rates than traditional loans
- Balloon payments may be required
- Title issues if not properly documented

Protection Strategy:

- Use a licensed title company
- Record the agreement with the county
- Verify the seller's ownership and mortgage status

Seller financing is a creative solution that reflects God's ability to provide outside the system. It's favor through relationship, not just regulation.

Creative Deals – Thinking Outside the Mortgage Box

"See, I am doing a new thing! Now it springs up; do you not perceive it?" (Isaiah 43:19).

Beyond traditional financing, there are other creative ways to acquire property:

- **Subject-to deals**: You take over the seller's existing mortgage
- **Wraparound mortgages**: You pay the seller, who continues paying the bank
- **Partnership purchases**: You co-buy with a trusted partner or investor

- **Land contracts**: You pay monthly until the deed transfers

These strategies require wisdom, legal counsel, and prayer. They're not for everyone—but they can be powerful tools for those called to build in unconventional ways.

Final Word: Steward the Strategy, Not Just the Opportunity

"The plans of the diligent lead surely to abundance, but everyone who is hasty comes only to poverty" (Proverbs 21:5).

Whether it's a 0% interest offer or a creative financing deal, discernment is key. Don't be dazzled by the headline—read the fine print, seek counsel, and pray for clarity. God doesn't just provide opportunities—He provides wisdom to steward them.

Let every deal you enter reflect your values, your vision, and your faith. You're not just acquiring property—you're building legacy. And the foundation must be truth.

***

Section 3: The Hidden Costs of Home Financing – What They Don't Tell You About Mortgage Payments and Land Value

The Deception of "Fixed" Costs

"The prudent see danger and take refuge, but the simple keep going and pay the penalty" (Proverbs 27:12).

Many aspiring homeowners step into financing agreements believing their monthly mortgage payments will remain stable. They're told they've locked in a "fixed rate," and they budget accordingly. But months later, they're blindsided by rising payments—not because the interest rate changed, but because the property taxes and insurance premiums did. What most banks, builders, and even realtors fail to explain is that the value of the land is reassessed once the home is built, triggering a new tax calculation that significantly increases the escrow portion of the mortgage.

This isn't just a financial oversight—it's a spiritual warning. God calls His people to walk in wisdom, not assumption. Before you build, you must count the cost (Luke 14:28). And before you borrow, you must understand the full picture.

Land Value vs. Improved Property Value

"By wisdom a house is built, and through understanding it is established" (Proverbs 24:3).

When you purchase land, the county or city assesses its value based on its current state—vacant, unimproved, and often taxed at a lower rate. But once a home is constructed, the property undergoes a new assessment. The land is now "improved," and the value skyrockets. This triggers:

- Higher property taxes
- Increased escrow payments
- Adjusted insurance premiums
- A recalculated monthly mortgage payment

Most lenders bundle taxes and insurance into your monthly payment through escrow. So even if your loan's interest rate is fixed, your total payment is not. This is why many homeowners see their mortgage jump by hundreds of dollars after the first year.

Builders and realtors often gloss over this reality, focusing on the excitement of new construction. But wisdom demands clarity. You must know what you're stepping into—not just what you're stepping onto.

What Financial Institutions Don't Want You to Know

"The Lord detests dishonest scales, but accurate weights find favor with Him" (Proverbs 11:1).

Banks profit from your ignorance. The more you borrow, the more they earn in interest, fees, and servicing. They rarely explain:

- How escrow recalculations work
- That "fixed rate" doesn't mean "fixed payment"
- That new construction triggers reassessment
- That insurance premiums rise with property value

Builders benefit from quick closings and inflated appraisals. Realtors earn commissions based on sale price, not long-term affordability. The system is designed to move you through the process—not to educate you.

But God's economy is different. He calls us to steward, not stumble. To build with understanding, not impulse. To possess the land with peace, not panic.

Why Going a Different Route Might Be in Your Best Interest

"Stand at the crossroads and look; ask for the ancient paths, ask where the good way is, and walk in it..." (Jeremiah 6:16).

Alternative paths to homeownership may offer more transparency, flexibility, and peace. These include:

- **Buying land and building in phases** with cash or small loans
- **Lease-to-own agreements** that allow you to occupy while building equity
- **Seller financing** with direct terms and no escrow surprises
- **Tiny homes or modular units** placed on land with lower tax impact
- **Community land trusts** that stabilize property taxes and promote

affordability

These routes require patience, planning, and prayer—but they often lead to greater financial freedom and spiritual peace. You're not just buying a house—you're building a legacy. And legacy must be built on truth.

Final Word: Build with Revelation, Not Just Excitement

"Unless the Lord builds the house, the builders labor in vain" (Psalm 127:1).

Home financing is full of hidden traps—but God offers wisdom to navigate them. Don't be swayed by surface-level promises. Ask questions. Read the fine print. Seek counsel. And consider alternative paths that align with your values and vision.

Your home should be a place of rest, not regret. Let every brick be laid in truth. Let every payment reflect stewardship. And let your journey into homeownership be guided not by hype, but by Heaven.

***

Buying land and building in phases with cash or small loans can offer greater financial control and spiritual peace. However, burying a family member on your land does *not* automatically exempt you from property taxes unless you formally designate and record the area as a private cemetery.

Section 4: Building in Phases and Burying with Purpose – Land Stewardship and Legacy with Wisdom

Building Slowly, Building Strong

"By wisdom a house is built, and through understanding it is established" (Proverbs 24:3).

In a world driven by urgency and debt, building your home in phases with cash or small loans is a radical act of stewardship. It allows you to avoid overwhelming mortgage payments, reduce interest burdens, and maintain control over your timeline and materials. This method reflects the biblical principle of counting the cost before building (Luke 14:28), ensuring that each step is taken with clarity and conviction.

Benefits of Building in Phases:

- No long-term mortgage debt
- Flexibility to adjust plans as needed
- Ability to pay cash for materials and labor
- Opportunity to build as resources allow

Whether you start with a foundation, a tiny home, or a modular unit, each phase becomes a testimony of faith and provision. You're not just constructing a house—you're cultivating legacy.

Using Small Loans Strategically

"The borrower is slave to the lender" (Proverbs 22:7).

While cash is ideal, small loans can be used wisely to fund specific phases—such as installing plumbing, purchasing materials, or securing permits. These loans should be short-term, low-interest, and paid off quickly to avoid compounding debt.

Strategy:

- Use credit unions or community banks
- Borrow only what you can repay within 12–24 months
- Avoid high-interest personal loans or credit cards

- Track every expense and repayment

This approach honors God's call to be lenders, not perpetual borrowers (Deuteronomy 15:6). It's about using tools, not being trapped by them.

Burial on Private Land – Tax Implications and Legal Truth

"Precious in the sight of the Lord is the death of His faithful servants" (Psalm 116:15).

Some families choose to bury loved ones on their own land as an act of legacy and spiritual honor. While this is legal in many states (with proper permits and zoning compliance), it does *not* automatically exempt the property from taxes.

Key Facts:

- A single burial does *not* change the property's tax status.
- To qualify for a tax exemption, you must legally designate a portion of the land as a *private cemetery.*
- This requires surveying the burial plot, recording it with the county, and ensuring it is used *exclusively* for burial purposes.
- Only the designated cemetery portion may be exempt—not the entire property.

Legal Steps:

- Check state and local zoning laws
- Obtain a burial-transit permit and death certificate
- Record the cemetery designation with the county deed office
- Ensure the land is not within city limits (in some states)

This is a sacred act—but it must be done with legal clarity. God honors legacy, but He also calls us to walk in truth and order (1 Corinthians 14:40).

Final Word: Stewardship Is Both Spiritual and Practical

"The land must not be sold permanently, because the land is mine and you reside in my land as foreigners and strangers" (Leviticus 25:23).

Buying land, building in phases, and honoring your loved ones through burial are deeply spiritual acts. But they also require practical wisdom.

Avoiding debt, understanding tax law, and navigating zoning regulations are part of your testimony. You're not just acquiring property—you're stewarding promise.

Let every brick, every phase, and every burial reflect the glory of a God who builds legacy through obedience, not haste.

Sources: LegalClarity – Home Burial and Property Taxes Kershaw, Vititoe & Jedinak – Tax-Exempt Burial Grounds

***

You can use retirement accounts like IRAs and 401(k)s to buy your first home, but it requires wisdom and strategy to avoid penalties and long-term financial setbacks. The IRS allows certain exceptions for first-time homebuyers, but each account type has specific rules.

Section 5: Using Retirement Accounts to Buy Your First Home – Redeeming What Was Set Aside for a Greater Purpose

When the Seed Becomes the Harvest

"Cast your bread upon the waters, for you will find it after many days" (Ecclesiastes 11:1).

Retirement accounts are designed to provide for your future—but sometimes, the future begins with a home. For first-time buyers, tapping into an IRA or 401(k) can be a strategic way to fund a down payment or closing costs. While these accounts are meant for long-term growth, the IRS allows specific exceptions that let you access funds without penalty when purchasing your first home. This is a moment of redemption—using what was stored for later to build legacy now.

Using an IRA – Grace for the First-Time Homebuyer

"The Lord will open the heavens, the storehouse of His bounty, to bless all the work of your hands" (Deuteronomy 28:12).

If you have a traditional or Roth IRA, the IRS allows you to withdraw up to **$10,000 penalty-free** for a first-time home purchase. This applies to you, your spouse, or even a child or grandchild buying their first home.

Key Points:

- You must use the funds for a primary residence.
- The $10,000 limit is per person—married couples can withdraw up to $20,000.
- You'll still owe income tax on withdrawals from a traditional IRA.
- Roth IRA contributions can be withdrawn tax-free, but earnings may be taxed if the account is under five years old.

This is a biblical picture of stored provision—like Joseph setting aside grain for a future famine (Genesis 41:48–49). What you saved in faith can now be used to build your foundation.

Using a 401(k) – Borrowing from Your Future with Caution

"The borrower is slave to the lender" (Proverbs 22:7).

With a 401(k), you have two options: **withdrawal** or **loan**. A withdrawal before age 59½ typically incurs a 10% penalty and income tax. However, some plans allow loans up to **$50,000 or 50% of your vested balance**, whichever is less.

Why a Loan May Be Better:

- No penalty or income tax
- You repay yourself with interest
- Doesn't affect your credit score or debt-to-income ratio

Risks:

- You must repay within five years
- If you leave your job, the loan may become due immediately
- You stop contributing to your 401(k) until the loan is repaid

This is a strategy of stewardship—not recklessness. Like Nehemiah rebuilding the wall with limited resources (Nehemiah 2:20), you must count the cost and build wisely.

Spiritual Wisdom for Financial Decisions

"Plans fail for lack of counsel, but with many advisers they succeed" (Proverbs 15:22).

Using retirement funds to buy a home is not for everyone. It can reduce your future earnings and delay retirement goals. But for those who've prayed, planned, and prepared, it can be a breakthrough strategy. Seek financial counsel, understand the tax implications, and move forward only if it aligns with your long-term vision.

Final Word: Build the House, Honor the Future

"By wisdom a house is built, and through understanding it is established" (Proverbs 24:3).

Your retirement account is more than money—it's a seed. And sometimes, God calls you to plant that seed early to build something greater. Whether through an IRA withdrawal or a 401(k) loan, use what you've stored to step into ownership with faith, strategy, and stewardship. Let your home be a testimony of provision, not panic. And let your future still flourish—because the God who gave you the seed will also give you the harvest.

Sources: Zillow – Using Your 401(k) to Buy a House U.S. News – Using Your IRA to Buy a House Mortgage Research – Retirement Funds and Home Buying.

***

Section 6: The Secrets of Inheriting Family Homes Through a Trust – Preserving Legacy with Wisdom and Spiritual Foresight

Inheritance Is a Covenant, Not Just a Transaction

"A good person leaves an inheritance for their children's children..." (Proverbs 13:22).

When it comes to passing down property, especially family homes, many assume a will is the best or only option. But in truth, a trust offers a more secure, private, and strategic way to transfer ownership across generations. Wills must go through probate—a public, often costly legal process that can delay access to the home and expose the estate to disputes. Trusts, on the other hand, bypass probate entirely, allowing heirs to inherit property smoothly, quietly, and with fewer complications.

This chapter reveals the spiritual and practical wisdom behind using a trust to inherit family homes. It's not just about legal structure—it's about preserving legacy, protecting peace, and honoring the covenant of generational blessing.

Why a Trust Is Better Than a Will for Property Transfer

"Plans fail for lack of counsel, but with many advisers they succeed" (Proverbs 15:22).

A will outlines your wishes, but it must be validated by a court. This means:

- Probate court involvement
- Public record of assets and heirs
- Potential for family disputes
- Delays in accessing or selling the home

A trust, however, is a legal entity that holds the property while the original owner is alive and transfers it automatically upon death. No court. No delay. No drama.

Benefits of a Trust:

- Immediate transfer of ownership
- Privacy—no public record
- Protection from creditors and legal challenges
- Ability to set conditions (e.g., age, use, maintenance)

This reflects God's wisdom in structure. Just as He established covenants with Abraham, Isaac, and Jacob, a trust is a modern-day covenant that secures inheritance with clarity and peace.

How a Trust Works in Real Estate Inheritance

"The boundary lines have fallen for me in pleasant places; surely I have a delightful inheritance" (Psalm 16:6).

When a family home is placed in a trust, the trust becomes the legal owner. The person creating the trust (the grantor) names beneficiaries and a trustee to manage the property. Upon the grantor's death, the trustee transfers the home to the beneficiaries without court approval.

Steps to Set It Up:

1. Create a revocable living trust with an estate attorney
2. Title the home in the name of the trust
3. Name beneficiaries and successor trustees
4. Include instructions for use, sale, or occupancy
5. Keep the trust updated as family dynamics change

This is stewardship in action—planning ahead to protect what God has entrusted to your family.

Spiritual Implications of Trust-Based Inheritance

"The Lord will make you the head, not the tail. If you pay attention to the commands... you will always be at the top, never at the bottom" (Deuteronomy 28:13).

Using a trust to pass down property is more than a legal move—it's a prophetic act. It reflects foresight, order, and honor. It prevents strife, confusion, and division. It allows heirs to receive their inheritance in peace, without the burden of legal battles or financial strain.

This is how Kingdom families build legacy. Not just with wealth, but with wisdom. Not just with assets, but with alignment.

Final Word: Protect the Promise, Preserve the Peace

"Blessed is the one who finds wisdom, and the one who gets understanding" (Proverbs 3:13).

If you've been entrusted with a family home—or hope to pass one down—consider a trust. It's the hidden key to inheritance that many overlook. It protects your heirs, preserves your wishes, and honors the biblical principle of legacy.

Don't wait for probate to decide your family's future. Build the trust. Secure the home. And let your inheritance reflect the order, peace, and blessing of Heaven.

Chapter 9: Funding Secrets of the Wealthy – Unlocking the Strategies Hidden in Plain Sight

Wealth Is Built, Not Just Inherited

"The wealth of the wicked is stored up for the righteous" (Proverbs 13:22).

Many people assume that the wealthy simply inherit their riches or stumble into fortune. But in reality, wealth is often built through strategic access to funding, leveraging systems, and multiplying resources. The wealthy don't just earn—they position. They understand how to use credit, capital, and connections to fund their ventures, protect their assets, and expand their influence. This chapter reveals the hidden strategies they use—and how you can apply them with wisdom, integrity, and faith.

God doesn't just bless with provision—He blesses with insight. The secrets of the wealthy are not reserved for the elite; they are available to those who seek, ask, and knock (Matthew 7:7).

Secret 1: Leveraging Other People's Money (OPM)

*"You may say to yourself, 'My power and the strength of my hands have produced this wealth for me,' but remember the Lord your God, for it is He who gives you the ability to produce wealth..." (Deuteronomy 8:17–18).

Wealthy individuals rarely use their own money to fund projects. They use OPM—Other People's Money—through business credit, investor capital, and strategic partnerships. They understand that money is a tool, not a trophy. By leveraging lines of credit, grants, and low-interest loans, they multiply their reach without draining their reserves.

How You Can Apply It:

- Build business credit separate from personal credit
- Apply for grants and funding through local and federal programs
- Use strategic partnerships to share costs and expand impact

This is not manipulation—it's multiplication. It's the principle of stewardship, using what's available to produce more.

Secret 2: Asset-Based Lending and Collateral Strategy

*"To everyone who has, more will be given, and he will have an abundance..." (Matthew 25:29).

The wealthy understand that assets—real estate, vehicles, stocks, and even intellectual property—can be used as collateral to secure funding. They don't just own things; they leverage them. By pledging assets, they gain access to larger loans, better terms, and faster approvals.

How You Can Apply It:

- Use paid-off vehicles or property to secure small business loans
- Monetize intellectual property (books, courses, trademarks)
- Explore securities-backed lines of credit

This is the principle of increase—using what you have to unlock what you need.

Secret 3: Strategic Tax Positioning and Entity Formation

*"Render to Caesar what is Caesar's, and to God what is God's" (Matthew 22:21).

Wealthy individuals don't just earn—they structure. They form LLCs, S-corps, and trusts to protect their income, reduce tax liability, and qualify for business funding. They understand that the tax code rewards those who build, invest, and employ. By positioning themselves as entities, they access deductions, credits, and funding streams unavailable to W-2 earners.

How You Can Apply It:

- Form an LLC to separate personal and business finances
- Track expenses and use accounting software
- Consult a tax strategist to maximize deductions

This is not avoidance—it's alignment. It's using the laws of the land to walk in wisdom and stewardship.

Secret 4: Relationship Capital and Insider Access

*"A man who has friends must himself be friendly, but there is a friend who sticks closer than a brother" (Proverbs 18:24).

Wealthy individuals understand the power of relationships. They network with lenders, investors, and advisors who open doors to funding others never hear about. They attend private events, join mastermind groups, and build trust with gatekeepers. Their access is relational, not just financial.

How You Can Apply It:

- Join local business associations or faith-based entrepreneur groups
- Build relationships with bankers, grant officers, and mentors
- Serve others generously—favor flows through honor

This is the principle of divine connection—God uses people to release provision.

Final Word: You're Not Locked Out—You're Being Positioned

*"I will give you hidden treasures, riches stored in secret places..." (Isaiah 45:3).

The funding secrets of the wealthy are not reserved for the elite—they're available to the diligent, the faithful, and the strategic. You don't need millions to start—you need wisdom, positioning, and obedience. God is not just your provider—He's your strategist. He will show you how to access what's hidden, multiply what's small, and build what lasts.

Step into these secrets with faith. Apply them with integrity. And let your journey reflect the truth that wealth is not just about money—it's about mission, multiplication, and Kingdom impact.

***

The wealthiest individuals and corporations often use business credit, EINs, and shelf corporations to access funding, build credibility, and protect personal assets—all without relying on personal credit. These tools reflect strategic stewardship and legal positioning that align with biblical principles of wisdom, multiplication, and legacy.

Section 1: How the 1% Use Business Credit, EINs, and Shelf Corporations – Unlocking Financial Favor Through Structure and Strategy

Wealth Is Structured, Not Just Earned

"By wisdom a house is built, and through understanding it is established; through knowledge its rooms are filled with rare and beautiful treasures" (Proverbs 24:3–4).

The top 1% don't just make money—they structure it. They understand that wealth flows through systems, not just effort. Business credit, EINs (Employer Identification Numbers), and shelf corporations are tools they use to separate personal liability from business opportunity, access large lines of credit, and fast-track credibility with lenders and partners. These strategies aren't reserved for the elite—they're available to anyone willing to learn, apply, and build with wisdom.

Business Credit – Building Without Personal Risk

"The borrower is slave to the lender" (Proverbs 22:7).

Business credit allows entrepreneurs to borrow money, secure vendor accounts, and build financial history using their company's profile—not their personal credit. The wealthy use business credit to:

- Fund operations without personal guarantees
- Protect their personal assets
- Qualify for high-limit credit cards and loans
- Establish credibility with suppliers and partners

How to Start:

- Form an LLC or corporation
- Obtain an EIN from the IRS
- Open a business bank account
- Register with Dun & Bradstreet to get a DUNS number
- Apply for Net-30 vendor accounts (e.g., Uline, Grainger)

This is stewardship in action—building financial capacity without compromising personal peace.

EINs – The Identity of the Business

"Give to Caesar what is Caesar's, and to God what is God's" (Matthew 22:21).

An EIN is the business equivalent of a Social Security number. It's used to file taxes, open bank accounts, and apply for credit. The wealthy use EINs to:

- Create multiple business entities for different ventures
- Separate income streams for tax efficiency
- Qualify for grants and government contracts
- Build layered protection and privacy

Each EIN represents a new opportunity—a new vessel for favor, funding, and function.

Shelf Corporations – Fast-Tracking Credibility and Capital

"The wealth of the wicked is stored up for the righteous" (Proverbs 13:22).

A shelf corporation is a pre-registered business that has aged without activity. The wealthy purchase these entities to gain instant credibility, bypass startup restrictions, and qualify for funding that requires years of history.

Benefits:

- Immediate access to aged business credit
- Faster approval for loans and contracts
- Enhanced trust with lenders and clients
- Ability to secure funding without personal credit checks

Caution:

- Work with reputable brokers
- Verify the corporation's history and standing
- Activate and build credit properly

Shelf corporations are like vessels waiting to be filled. When used ethically, they accelerate growth and multiply impact.

Final Word: Structure Unlocks Stewardship

"I will give you hidden treasures, riches stored in secret places..." (Isaiah 45:3).

The 1% don't just work harder—they build smarter. They use business credit, EINs, and shelf corporations to unlock funding, protect assets, and expand influence. These tools are not shortcuts—they're strategies. And they reflect the biblical principle that wisdom builds the house, not hustle alone.

You don't need millions to start—you need structure. Begin with one entity. Build your credit. Position your business. And let your financial journey reflect the order, favor, and legacy of the Kingdom.

Sources: Forbes – Shelf Corporations as a Credit Workaround Derrick Whitehead – Guide to Shelf Corporations with Credit Packages

***

Section 2: Shelf Corporations as a Credit Strategy – Accelerating Access Through Aged Authority

Wisdom Builds What Time Strengthens

"To everyone who has, more will be given, and he will have an abundance..." (Matthew 25:29).

In the realm of business credit, time is a currency. Lenders, vendors, and financial institutions often favor companies with longevity—even if that company has yet to generate revenue. Shelf corporations, also known as aged corporations, are entities that were formed months or years ago but have remained inactive. The wealthy use these corporations to fast-track credibility, qualify for funding, and bypass the limitations of startup status. It's not deception—it's positioning. And when used ethically, it reflects the biblical principle of multiplying what already exists.

This chapter explores how shelf corporations function as a credit strategy, how to activate them properly, and how they align with Kingdom principles of stewardship, acceleration, and favor.

What Is a Shelf Corporation?

"The plans of the diligent lead surely to abundance..." (Proverbs 21:5).

A shelf corporation is a legally formed business entity that has been "shelved"—left inactive for a period of time. It has no assets, liabilities, or operations, but it does have age. That age becomes a powerful asset when seeking business credit, contracts, or partnerships.

Benefits of Shelf Corporations:

- Instant credibility with lenders and vendors
- Eligibility for funding that requires 2+ years of business history
- Faster approval for government contracts and corporate leases
- Enhanced trust with clients and suppliers

This is strategic stewardship—using what's already built to unlock what's yet to come.

Shelf Corporations and Business Credit

"Enlarge the place of your tent... do not hold back; lengthen your cords, strengthen your stakes" (Isaiah 54:2).

Business credit is built on time, trade history, and financial behavior. Shelf corporations allow you to skip the "new business" phase and begin building credit immediately. Once activated, you can:

- Open a business bank account
- Apply for Net-30 vendor accounts
- Register with Dun & Bradstreet
- Secure business credit cards and lines of credit

Important Steps:

- Verify the corporation's good standing with the state
- Update the registered agent and business address
- File any necessary annual reports or reinstatements
- Begin building real trade activity to support the aged profile

This is how the 1% accelerate access—they don't wait for time to pass, they purchase time already passed.

Ethical Use and Spiritual Integrity

"Better a little with righteousness than much gain with injustice" (Proverbs 16:8).

Shelf corporations must be used with integrity. They are not a license to misrepresent your business history or deceive lenders. Instead, they are a tool to position your business for growth, provided you activate them properly and build real operations behind the name.

Use with Integrity:

- Disclose the corporation's history when required
- Avoid using shelf corps for fraudulent credit applications
- Build real value and impact through the entity

God honors truth, even in strategy. The goal is not to manipulate systems, but to steward opportunities with wisdom and righteousness.

Final Word: Redeem Time, Multiply Favor

"I will restore to you the years the locusts have eaten..." (Joel 2:25).

Shelf corporations are a prophetic picture of redeemed time. They allow you to step into opportunities that would otherwise take years to qualify for. When used ethically, they reflect God's ability to accelerate your assignment, multiply your reach, and establish your business with favor.

Don't just build from scratch—build from strength. Let the age of the entity become a platform for new beginnings. And let your business journey reflect the wisdom, acceleration, and integrity of the Kingdom.

***

Section 3: How to Get Loans Even with Poor Credit – Unlocking Favor Through Strategy and Stewardship

God's Grace Makes a Way Where Credit Can't

"For the Lord God is a sun and shield; the Lord bestows favor and honor; no good thing does He withhold from those whose walk is blameless" (Psalm 84:11).

Poor credit doesn't have to mean a closed door. While traditional lenders may judge based on numbers, God opens doors based on faith, wisdom, and preparation. There are still ways to access funding—even with a low score—if you understand how to position yourself, present your case, and pursue the right lenders. This chapter reveals practical strategies and spiritual truths to help you secure loans, rebuild trust, and walk in financial restoration.

Step 1: Know Where You Stand and Clean What You Can

"My people are destroyed for lack of knowledge..." (Hosea 4:6).

Before applying for any loan, pull your credit reports from all three bureaus (Experian, Equifax, and TransUnion). Look for:

- Errors or outdated accounts
- Collections that can be settled or disputed
- High credit utilization that can be paid down
- Accounts you can bring current

Even small improvements can raise your score and increase your chances of approval. This is the principle of stewardship—taking responsibility for what's in your hands before asking for more (Luke 16:10).

Step 2: Seek Lenders Who Look Beyond the Score

"Man looks at the outward appearance, but the Lord looks at the heart" (1 Samuel 16:7).

Not all lenders rely solely on credit scores. Some consider your income, employment history, and overall financial behavior. These include:

- Credit unions and community banks

- Online lenders with flexible underwriting
- Peer-to-peer lending platforms
- CDFIs (Community Development Financial Institutions)

These lenders often offer personal loans, auto loans, or small business funding—even to those with poor credit—if you can demonstrate stability and intent.

Tip: Write a personal statement explaining your credit history and how you've turned things around. Honesty builds trust.

Step 3: Use Collateral or a Co-Signer to Strengthen Your Case

"Two are better than one... if either of them falls down, one can help the other up" (Ecclesiastes 4:9–10).

If your credit is weak, you can offer collateral (like a vehicle or savings account) or ask someone with stronger credit to co-sign. This reduces the lender's risk and increases your approval odds.

Options Include:

- Secured personal loans (backed by savings or assets)
- Title loans (use with caution and only from reputable lenders)
- Co-signed loans (ensure both parties understand the responsibility)

This is a picture of partnership and accountability—walking together to reach a goal.

Step 4: Consider Credit-Builder Loans and Alternative Financing

"Do not despise these small beginnings, for the Lord rejoices to see the work begin" (Zechariah 4:10).

Credit-builder loans are designed to help you rebuild while saving. You make monthly payments into a locked account, and once the loan is repaid, you receive the funds—plus a stronger credit profile.

Other Creative Options:

- Pay advance apps (Earnin, Brigit)
- Buy-now-pay-later platforms (for small purchases)
- Business microloans or grants (if self-employed)

These tools may not offer large sums, but they build momentum. And in the Kingdom, small steps lead to great harvests.

Final Word: Faith Opens Doors, Strategy Keeps Them Open

"Commit your works to the Lord, and your plans will be established" (Proverbs 16:3).

Getting a loan with poor credit is possible—but it requires faith, preparation, and persistence. Don't be discouraged by rejection. Instead, use it as redirection. Strengthen your profile. Seek the right partners. And trust that God will provide what you need, when you need it.

You are not disqualified. You are being refined. And as you walk in wisdom, the same systems that once denied you will become channels of favor. Let your testimony be one of restoration, not just approval. Let your loan be a tool—not a trap. And let your journey reflect the goodness of a God who redeems, rebuilds, and restores.

***

Section 4: FreedomVoice: A Strategic Tool for Business Communication

What Is FreedomVoice?

"Let your conversation be always full of grace, seasoned with salt, so that you may know how to answer everyone" (Colossians 4:6).

FreedomVoice is a virtual phone service provider that specializes in toll-free (800) and local business numbers. It's designed for entrepreneurs and small businesses who want to project professionalism, manage calls efficiently, and stay mobile. With FreedomVoice, you can set up a business line that routes calls to your cell phone, office, or voicemail—without needing a physical phone system.

This reflects the biblical principle of stewardship—using modern tools to manage your business with excellence and clarity.

Key Features of FreedomVoice 800 Numbers

"Whatever you do, work at it with all your heart, as working for the Lord..." (Colossians 3:23).

FreedomVoice offers several features that make it ideal for growing businesses:

- **Instant Setup**: Get your 800 number activated within minutes.
- **Virtual Receptionist**: Automatically answers and routes calls based on your preferences.
- **Call Forwarding**: Direct calls to any number—mobile, office, or team member.
- **Voicemail to Email**: Receive voicemails as audio files in your inbox.
- **No Contracts**: Month-to-month service with no long-term commitment.
- **Mobile App**: Manage calls and messages from anywhere.

These features help you stay organized, responsive, and professional—reflecting the excellence God calls us to walk in.

Pricing Plans

FreedomVoice offers three main plans:

- **Start Plan**: $9.95/month for 400 minutes
- **Edge Plan**: $19.95/month for 1,200 minutes
- **Max Plan**: $29.95/month for unlimited minutes

Each plan includes access to the virtual phone system, voicemail, call routing, and customer support. You can also start with a **30-day free trial** to test the service before committing.

Why It Matters for Kingdom Entrepreneurs

"Let all things be done decently and in order" (1 Corinthians 14:40).

Having a dedicated 800 number helps separate your personal life from your business, builds trust with customers, and positions your brand for growth. It's a tool of order, clarity, and professionalism—especially important for those called to serve with excellence in ministry and marketplace.

Whether you're launching a new venture or expanding your reach, FreedomVoice equips you to communicate with confidence and integrity.

Sources: You can learn more or sign up at FreedomVoice's official site.

Part IV: Protect & Prosper – Securing What God Has Given and Multiplying It with Wisdom

Stewardship Is Protection, Prosperity Is Purpose

"The blessing of the Lord brings wealth, without painful toil for it" (Proverbs 10:22).

Prosperity is not just about increase—it's about protection. In the Kingdom, wealth is not measured by accumulation alone, but by how well it's stewarded, shielded, and multiplied for generational impact. Part IV is about guarding what God has entrusted to you—your home, your credit, your business, your legacy—and positioning it to prosper. This is where spiritual discernment meets financial strategy. It's not just about getting more; it's about keeping what you've gained and growing it with integrity.

Protecting Your Credit and Identity

"A good name is more desirable than great riches; to be esteemed is better than silver or gold" (Proverbs 22:1).

Your credit profile is part of your financial identity. It reflects your reputation in the marketplace. Protecting it means monitoring your reports, disputing errors, and guarding against fraud. Use tools like credit freezes, fraud alerts, and secure passwords to shield your financial name.

Strategy:

- Check your credit reports monthly
- Use identity theft protection services
- Avoid co-signing for others without legal safeguards
- Keep your financial documents secure

This is spiritual warfare in the financial realm—guarding your name, your access, and your testimony.

Protecting Your Assets Through Legal Structure

"Plans are established by counsel; by wise guidance wage war" (Proverbs 20:18).

Wealthy individuals protect their assets through legal entities—LLCs, trusts, insurance policies, and contracts. These tools shield your home, business, and intellectual property from lawsuits, taxes, and unexpected loss.

Key Tools:

- Form an LLC to separate personal and business liability
- Create a living trust to pass down property without probate
- Use umbrella insurance to cover gaps in protection
- Trademark your brand and copyright your content

This is not fear—it's foresight. God calls us to build with wisdom, not just passion.

Prosperity Through Multiplication, Not Just Accumulation

"He who had received five talents went at once and traded with them, and he made five more talents" (Matthew 25:16).

Prosperity is not just about saving—it's about multiplying. Invest wisely. Start businesses. Build credit. Use what you have to produce more. The parable of the talents teaches us that God rewards those who multiply what He gives—not those who bury it in fear.

Multiplication Strategy:

- Use business credit to fund income-generating ventures
- Invest in real estate or land with long-term value
- Create digital products that scale (courses, books, designs)
- Partner with others to expand your reach

This is Kingdom economics—where stewardship leads to overflow.

Final Word: Guard the Garden, Grow the Harvest

"The Lord will make you the head, not the tail. If you pay attention to His commands... you will always be at the top, never at the bottom" (Deuteronomy 28:13).

Part IV is your call to protect and prosper. Guard what God has given you—your credit, your home, your business, your name. Then grow it. Multiply it. Use it to bless others and build legacy. You are not just a consumer—you are a cultivator. You are not just surviving—you are stewarding.

Let your protection be strategic. Let your prosperity be purposeful. And let your journey reflect the wisdom, favor, and abundance of a God who gives seed to the sower and multiplies the harvest.

Chapter 10: Identity Theft, Credit Freezes & Fraud Protection – Guarding What God Has Entrusted

Protecting Your Name Is Protecting Your Legacy

"A good name is more desirable than great riches; to be esteemed is better than silver or gold" (Proverbs 22:1).

In today's digital age, identity theft is more than a financial inconvenience—it's a spiritual attack on your name, your reputation, and your stewardship. When someone steals your identity, they're not just accessing your credit—they're attempting to hijack the fruit of your labor and the testimony of your integrity. God calls us to guard what He's entrusted to us, and that includes our financial identity. This chapter equips you with the tools to freeze your credit, detect fraud, and protect your name with wisdom and vigilance.

Identity Theft – The Silent Violation

"The thief comes only to steal and kill and destroy; I have come that they may have life..." (John 10:10).

Identity theft occurs when someone uses your personal information—like your Social Security number, bank account, or credit card—to commit fraud. It can lead to:

- Unauthorized loans or credit cards
- Damaged credit scores
- Legal complications
- Emotional stress and financial loss

This is a spiritual wake-up call. Just as we guard our hearts, we must guard our financial gates. The enemy seeks to steal, but God gives us authority to secure what's ours.

Credit Freezes – Locking the Gate Before the Enemy Enters

"The prudent see danger and take refuge, but the simple keep going and pay the penalty" (Proverbs 27:12).

A credit freeze is one of the most powerful tools to prevent identity theft. It blocks lenders from accessing your credit report, making it nearly impossible for thieves to open new accounts in your name.

How to Freeze Your Credit:

- Contact all three bureaus: Experian, Equifax, and TransUnion
- Provide your name, SSN, date of birth, and address
- Receive a PIN or password to lift the freeze when needed

Freezing your credit doesn't affect your score or existing accounts—it simply locks the door to new ones. It's a proactive act of stewardship.

Fraud Alerts – Sounding the Alarm

"Be alert and of sober mind. Your enemy the devil prowls around like a roaring lion..." (1 Peter 5:8).

If you suspect your identity has been compromised, placing a fraud alert on your credit report warns lenders to verify your identity before issuing credit. It lasts for one year and can be renewed.

Steps to Activate:

- Contact one credit bureau—they'll notify the others
- Provide documentation of suspected fraud
- Monitor your credit reports regularly

This is your spiritual alarm system—alerting the watchmen and guarding the gates.

Additional Protection Strategies

"The wise store up knowledge, but the mouth of a fool invites ruin" (Proverbs 10:14).

Beyond freezes and alerts, consider these protective measures:

- Use identity theft protection services
- Shred sensitive documents before disposal
- Avoid public Wi-Fi for financial transactions
- Use strong, unique passwords and two-factor authentication
- Monitor bank and credit card statements weekly

These are not just habits—they're disciplines of stewardship. You're not just protecting data—you're protecting destiny.

Final Word: Guard the Garden of Your Financial Identity

"Above all else, guard your heart, for everything you do flows from it" (Proverbs 4:23).

Your financial identity is part of your spiritual assignment. It reflects your name, your labor, and your legacy. Don't leave it exposed. Freeze what needs freezing. Alert what needs watching. And protect what God has given you with diligence and discernment.

Let your credit reflect your character. Let your vigilance reflect your value. And let your protection reflect the wisdom of a God who never sleeps nor slumbers. You are not just a consumer—you are a steward. Guard the garden. Prosper in peace.

***

Section 1: How to Lock Down Your Credit – Guarding Your Financial Identity with Wisdom and Authority

Securing What God Has Entrusted

"Above all else, guard your heart, for everything you do flows from it" (Proverbs 4:23).

Just as we are called to guard our hearts, we must also guard our financial identity. In today's digital economy, your credit profile is a gateway to opportunity—but it's also a target for theft, fraud, and manipulation. Locking down your credit is a proactive act of stewardship. It's not fear—it's foresight. It's not paranoia—it's protection. This chapter walks you through how to secure your credit with wisdom, aligning your financial boundaries with the spiritual principle of guarding what God has entrusted to you.

Step 1: Place a Credit Freeze with All Three Bureaus

"The prudent see danger and take refuge, but the simple keep going and pay the penalty" (Proverbs 27:12).

A credit freeze prevents lenders from accessing your credit report, making it nearly impossible for identity thieves to open new accounts in your name. It's free, reversible, and one of the most effective ways to lock down your credit.

How to Do It:

- Contact Experian, Equifax, and TransUnion individually
- Provide your full name, Social Security number, date of birth, and address
- Receive a PIN or password to lift the freeze when needed

This is your spiritual firewall—blocking unauthorized access and preserving your financial integrity.

Step 2: Set Up Fraud Alerts

"Be alert and of sober mind. Your enemy the devil prowls around like a roaring lion..." (1 Peter 5:8).

Fraud alerts notify lenders to take extra steps to verify your identity before issuing credit. They're especially helpful if you suspect your information has been compromised.

Types of Alerts:

- Initial Fraud Alert (lasts one year)
- Extended Fraud Alert (lasts seven years, requires a police report or identity theft affidavit)

How to Activate:

- Contact one credit bureau—they'll notify the others
- Provide documentation and a statement of concern

This is your spiritual alarm system—sounding the warning before damage is done.

Step 3: Monitor Your Credit Reports Regularly

"Know well the condition of your flocks, and give attention to your herds" (Proverbs 27:23).

You're entitled to one free credit report per year from each bureau at AnnualCreditReport.com. . Monitoring your reports helps you catch errors, unauthorized accounts, and suspicious activity early.

What to Look For:

- Accounts you didn't open
- Hard inquiries you didn't authorize
- Incorrect personal information
- Late payments or collections that don't belong to you

This is diligence in action—watching over what God has placed in your care.

Step 4: Use Identity Theft Protection Tools

"The Lord is my refuge and my fortress, my God, in whom I trust" (Psalm 91:2).

Consider using services that offer real-time alerts, dark web monitoring, and insurance coverage for identity theft. These tools act as a second layer of defense, especially if you've been targeted before.

Popular Options:

- LifeLock
- Identity Guard
- Experian IdentityWorks
- Aura

These services reflect the principle of refuge—creating safe boundaries around your financial life.

Final Word: Lock It Down, Live Free

"The Lord will keep you from all harm—He will watch over your life" (Psalm 121:7).

Locking down your credit isn't about living in fear—it's about living in freedom. When your financial identity is secure, you can move forward with confidence, clarity, and peace. You're not just protecting a score—you're protecting a story. A testimony. A legacy.

Let your credit reflect your character. Let your boundaries reflect your wisdom. And let your protection reflect the authority of a God who watches over every detail of your life. Lock it down. Live free. Build legacy.

***

Section 2: What to Do If Your Identity Is Compromised – Restoring What the Enemy Tried to Steal

When the Thief Comes, God Still Restores

"The thief comes only to steal and kill and destroy; I have come that they may have life, and have it to the full" (John 10:10).

Identity theft is a violation—not just of your finances, but of your name, your trust, and your peace. When your identity is compromised, it can feel like your life has been invaded. But take heart: God is a restorer. He gives wisdom for recovery, authority to reclaim what was stolen, and peace that surpasses understanding. This chapter outlines the practical and spiritual steps to take when your identity has been compromised, so you can move from chaos to clarity, and from loss to restoration.

Step 1: Alert the Credit Bureaus Immediately

"The prudent see danger and take refuge..." (Proverbs 27:12).

As soon as you suspect identity theft, contact the three major credit bureaus—Experian, Equifax, and TransUnion—to place a fraud alert or credit freeze on your file. A fraud alert warns lenders to take extra steps to verify your identity before issuing credit. A credit freeze locks your report entirely, preventing new accounts from being opened.

Action Steps:

- Request a one-year fraud alert (free and renewable)
- Consider a credit freeze for stronger protection
- Obtain and review your credit reports for suspicious activity

This is your first line of defense—closing the gates to further intrusion.

Step 2: File a Report with the FTC and Local Authorities

"Speak up and judge fairly; defend the rights of the poor and needy" (Proverbs 31:9).

The Federal Trade Commission (FTC) provides a step-by-step recovery plan through IdentityTheft.gov. Filing a report creates a legal record of the theft, which you'll need to dispute fraudulent accounts and protect your rights.

Also:

- File a police report with your local department
- Keep copies of all reports and correspondence
- Notify your bank and creditors immediately

This is about reclaiming your authority. When the enemy comes in like a flood, the Spirit of the Lord raises a standard against him (Isaiah 59:19).

Step 3: Close or Freeze Affected Accounts

"Let all things be done decently and in order" (1 Corinthians 14:40).

Contact every financial institution where fraud occurred. Close compromised accounts and open new ones with fresh credentials. Change all passwords, enable two-factor authentication, and monitor your statements daily.

Don't Forget:

- Notify your utility providers, insurance companies, and service accounts
- Update your passwords and security questions
- Use a password manager to create strong, unique logins

This is about restoring order—resetting what was corrupted and securing what remains.

Step 4: Dispute Fraudulent Charges and Monitor Recovery

"Do not be overcome by evil, but overcome evil with good" (Romans 12:21).

Once you've reported the fraud, begin the process of disputing unauthorized charges and accounts. Send written disputes to credit bureaus and creditors, including copies of your FTC and police reports. Monitor your credit reports monthly to ensure fraudulent items are removed and no new ones appear.

Tools to Help:

- Credit monitoring services

- Identity theft insurance (if available)
- Legal aid or consumer protection agencies

This is your redemption process—step by step, reclaiming what was lost.

Final Word: God Restores What Was Stolen

"I will repay you for the years the locusts have eaten..." (Joel 2:25).

If your identity has been compromised, know this: you are not powerless. You are not alone. And you are not defeated. God is your defender, your restorer, and your shield. As you take these steps in the natural, trust Him to work in the supernatural. He will restore your name, your peace, and your financial standing.

Let this be your declaration: "What the enemy meant for evil, God is turning for my good" (Genesis 50:20). Rise up, take action, and walk in the authority and wisdom that belongs to you as a child of the King. Your identity is not just a number—it's a calling. And no thief can steal what God has sealed.

***

Section 3: Monitoring Tools and Legal Recourse – Staying Vigilant and Reclaiming What's Yours

Watchfulness Is a Form of Warfare

"Be alert and of sober mind. Your enemy the devil prowls around like a roaring lion looking for someone to devour" (1 Peter 5:8).

In the realm of financial stewardship, vigilance is not optional—it's essential. Identity theft, credit fraud, and unauthorized access are modern-day schemes that seek to undermine your credibility and steal your inheritance. But God calls His people to be watchful, wise, and equipped. Monitoring tools and legal recourse are part of your spiritual and practical defense strategy. They help you detect threats early, respond with authority, and recover what was stolen. This chapter explores how to use these tools effectively and how to stand on the Word when facing financial warfare.

Monitoring Tools – Your Watchtower in the Digital Age

"Know well the condition of your flocks, and give attention to your herds" (Proverbs 27:23).

Just as shepherds watch over their sheep, you must watch over your financial identity. Monitoring tools alert you to suspicious activity, changes in your credit report, and breaches of your personal data. These tools are your early warning system—giving you time to act before damage is done.

Recommended Tools:

- **Credit Karma**: Free credit monitoring and score tracking
- **Experian IdentityWorks**: Real-time alerts and dark web surveillance
- **LifeLock**: Comprehensive protection with insurance coverage
- **Aura**: All-in-one identity and financial monitoring
- **Bank and credit card alerts**: Enable notifications for transactions and logins

These tools reflect the principle of diligence—watching over what God has entrusted to you with care and consistency.

Legal Recourse – Reclaiming What Was Stolen

"He will make your righteous reward shine like the dawn, your vindication like the noonday sun" (Psalm 37:6).

If your identity has been compromised or your credit misused, you have legal rights. The law provides pathways to dispute fraudulent charges, restore your credit, and hold perpetrators accountable. But you must act swiftly and document everything.

Steps to Take:

- File a report with the **Federal Trade Commission (FTC)** at IdentityTheft.gov
- Submit a **police report** with your local department
- Dispute fraudulent accounts with all three credit bureaus
- Contact affected creditors and request account closures or freezes
- Consider hiring a consumer protection attorney if the damage is extensive

This is your moment of vindication. Just as David recovered all that was stolen at Ziklag (1 Samuel 30:18), you too can reclaim what the enemy tried to take.

Spiritual Authority in Legal Matters

"No weapon formed against you shall prosper, and every tongue which rises against you in judgment you shall condemn..." (Isaiah 54:17).

Legal recourse is not just about paperwork—it's about standing in your God-given authority. You are not helpless. You are not defeated. You are a steward of Kingdom resources, and Heaven backs your pursuit of justice. Pray over every document. Declare restoration over every report. And trust that God will go before you in every courtroom, phone call, and dispute.

Final Word: Stay Alert, Stand Firm, and Recover All

"Resist him, standing firm in the faith, because you know that the family of believers throughout the world is undergoing the same kind of sufferings" (1 Peter 5:9).

Monitoring tools help you stay alert. Legal recourse helps you stand firm. Together, they empower you to recover all. Don't ignore the signs. Don't delay the response. And don't underestimate your authority.

You are not just protecting your credit—you are protecting your calling. Let your vigilance be rooted in faith. Let your recovery be marked by favor. And let your testimony be one of restoration, righteousness, and divine justice.

Chapter 11: Booming Side Hustles – Turning Craigslist Gigs into Kingdom Enterprises

Craigslist gig work and service-based side hustles like junk hauling, moving, and lawn care are booming opportunities with low startup costs and high local demand. These businesses thrive on speed, reliability, and visibility—especially when marketed through platforms like Craigslist, Facebook Marketplace, and Nextdoor.

Don't Just Work—Build What Lasts

"Whatever you do, work at it with all your heart, as working for the Lord..." (Colossians 3:23).

Side hustles aren't just about extra income—they're about stewardship, strategy, and service. When you meet a local need with excellence, you create opportunity, influence, and legacy. Craigslist's "Gigs" section is a goldmine for finding short-term work and launching service-based businesses that can scale fast. Whether it's junk hauling, moving help, or lawn care, these ventures require minimal upfront investment and can grow into full-time income streams with the right systems and spiritual mindset.

Junk Hauling – Turning Trash into Treasure

"He raises the poor from the dust and lifts the needy from the ash heap" (Psalm 113:7).

Junk hauling is one of the most overlooked yet profitable side hustles. People will pay hundreds just to have clutter removed. Startup costs are low—a trailer, gloves, and a few tools—and Craigslist is full of homeowners, landlords, and contractors needing help.

Startup Tips:

- Use Craigslist and Facebook Marketplace to advertise
- Offer same-day service and bundle with pressure washing or donation drop-offs
- Partner with realtors and property managers for recurring jobs

One Reddit user made $2,000 in their first month using a $100 trailer and Craigslist leads. This is a business of speed, trust, and visibility.

Moving Services – Strength in Motion

"Carry each other's burdens, and in this way you will fulfill the law of Christ" (Galatians 6:2).

Moving help is always in demand—especially for local or last-minute jobs. Craigslist's "Labor" and "Gigs" sections often list requests for packing, lifting, and transport. You don't need a truck to start—just muscle, hustle, and a hand truck.

Growth Strategy:

- Start solo or with a partner
- Offer flat-rate pricing and weekend availability
- Upsell with furniture assembly or junk removal

This hustle builds trust fast—and repeat clients become your best marketing.

Lawn Care – Cultivating Profit and Peace

"He makes grass grow for the cattle, and plants for people to cultivate—bringing forth food from the earth" (Psalm 104:14).

Lawn care is a seasonal but scalable business. Craigslist and neighborhood apps are full of homeowners needing mowing, edging, and cleanup. Start with basic tools and expand into landscaping, fertilization, or leaf removal.

Keys to Success:

- Offer weekly or biweekly packages
- Use before-and-after photos to showcase your work
- Build a referral program for neighbors

This is a business of consistency—and consistency builds credibility.

Craigslist Gig Work – Your Launchpad to Legacy

"Do not despise these small beginnings, for the Lord rejoices to see the work begin" (Zechariah 4:10).

Craigslist isn't just a job board—it's a launchpad. Use it to:

- Test your services
- Build your client base
- Learn what people are willing to pay for

Every gig is a seed. Plant it with excellence, water it with faith, and watch God multiply it.

Sources: Reddit – I Started a Junk Hauling Business Side Hustle Nation – Junk Hauling Business Guide Big Money Methods – Junk Hauling as a Goldmine

Would you like help drafting Craigslist ad copy or a launch checklist for one of these businesses?

***

Section 1: Here's a curated list of simple, service-based side hustle businesses.

You can launch using gig apps like Craigslist, TaskRabbit, Thumbtack, Handy, and even Facebook Marketplace. These are high-demand, low-barrier opportunities that align with your entrepreneurial spirit and Kingdom mindset of serving with excellence.

Service-Based Side Hustles Using Gig Apps

1. Furniture Assembly & Installation

"Let all things be done decently and in order" (1 Corinthians 14:40).

- Assemble IKEA, Wayfair, or Amazon furniture
- Mount TVs, curtain rods, shelves, and artwork
- Use TaskRabbit or Handy to find clients
- Great for detail-oriented individuals with basic tools

2. Painting Services (Interior/Exterior)

"He has filled him with the Spirit of God... to design artistic works..." (Exodus 35:31–32).

- Offer room painting, touch-ups, or fence staining
- Start with Craigslist or Thumbtack listings
- Upsell with drywall patching or color consultations
- Requires brushes, rollers, drop cloths, and patience

3. Minor Home Repairs & Handyman Work

"By wisdom a house is built..." (Proverbs 24:3).

- Fix leaky faucets, replace light fixtures, patch drywall
- Use apps like Thumbtack or Nextdoor to advertise
- Offer hourly rates or flat fees for common tasks
- Ideal for those with basic carpentry or electrical skills

4. Smart Home Setup & Tech Help

"Daniel was found to have insight and intelligence..." (Daniel 5:12).

- Install Ring cameras, thermostats, Wi-Fi routers, or smart bulbs
- Help seniors or busy families set up devices
- Advertise on Facebook Marketplace or TaskRabbit
- Great for tech-savvy individuals with a teaching spirit

5. Cleaning Services (Residential or Move-Out)
"Create in me a clean heart, O God..." (Psalm 51:10).

- Offer deep cleaning, organizing, or post-renovation cleanup
- Use Craigslist, Handy, or local Facebook groups
- Bundle with junk removal or donation drop-offs
- Requires cleaning supplies and a reliable schedule

6. Yard Work & Landscaping
"He makes grass grow for the cattle, and plants for people to cultivate..." (Psalm 104:14).

- Mow lawns, trim hedges, rake leaves, or plant flowers
- Offer seasonal packages or one-time cleanups
- Use gig apps or door-to-door flyers in your neighborhood
- Start with basic tools and scale into full landscaping

7. Moving Help & Packing Services
"Carry each other's burdens..." (Galatians 6:2).

- Help load/unload trucks, pack boxes, or organize storage
- Use Craigslist's "Labor" section or TaskRabbit
- Offer flat-rate or hourly pricing
- Great for strong, reliable workers with a service mindset

8. Pressure Washing & Exterior Cleaning
"Wash me, and I shall be whiter than snow" (Psalm 51:7).

- Clean driveways, siding, decks, and fences
- Rent or invest in a pressure washer
- Advertise before-and-after photos on Facebook or Nextdoor

- Bundle with gutter cleaning or window washing

9. Pet Services (Walking, Sitting, Grooming)
"The righteous care for the needs of their animals..." (Proverbs 12:10).

- Offer dog walking, pet sitting, or basic grooming
- Use Rover or Craigslist to find clients
- Great for animal lovers with flexible schedules

10. Event Setup & Breakdown
"Prepare the way for the Lord..." (Isaiah 40:3).

- Help with chairs, tables, decorations, and cleanup
- Partner with local venues or event planners
- Use gig apps or offer services on wedding forums
- Ideal for weekends and seasonal work

***

Section 2: Let's build a side hustle that moves with purpose and multiplies with precision.

Whether it's a shipping service, medical courier business, or general delivery operation, these ventures are rooted in trust, timeliness, and stewardship. Below is a launch checklist followed by ad copy tailored for a **medical courier business**—a high-trust, high-impact niche that aligns beautifully with your values of service, excellence, and Kingdom authority.

Medical Courier Business Launch Checklist

"Write the vision and make it plain..." (Habakkuk 2:2)

Legal & Licensing

- Register your business (LLC recommended for liability protection)
- Obtain an EIN for business banking and credit
- Check state requirements for medical courier licensing or HIPAA compliance
- Secure business insurance (general liability + cargo coverage)

Equipment & Setup

- Reliable vehicle with climate control (if transporting specimens)
- GPS and route optimization app (RoadWarrior, Circuit, or OnFleet)
- Lockable containers for secure transport
- Branded uniform or ID badge for professionalism

Operations & Systems

- Create standard operating procedures (pickup, delivery, chain of custody)
- Set up invoicing and payment system (Square, QuickBooks, or Wave)

- Build relationships with local labs, clinics, pharmacies, and hospitals
- Offer same-day, scheduled, and emergency delivery options

Marketing & Outreach

- Create a simple website or landing page with contact form
- List services on Craigslist, Thumbtack, and Google Business Profile
- Network with healthcare providers and medical office managers
- Offer referral incentives for recurring clients

Sample Ad Copy: Medical Courier Service

Faithful. Fast. Secure. Your Trusted Medical Courier in Melbourne, FL

Are you a clinic, lab, or pharmacy in need of reliable specimen or prescription delivery? We specialize in **same-day, HIPAA-compliant medical courier services**—serving Melbourne and surrounding areas with speed, integrity, and care.

◈ Lab Specimen Transport ◈ Prescription Delivery ◈ Medical Equipment Drop-Off ◈ Emergency & Scheduled Routes ◈ Chain of Custody Documentation

We operate with excellence, discretion, and Kingdom values—because your mission matters.

Call or text [Your Business Name] at (XXX) XXX-XXXX ◈ Email: info@[yourdomain].com Visit: www.[yourdomain].com

"Whatever you do, work at it with all your heart, as working for the Lord..." (Colossians 3:23)

***

Section 3: Side Hustle Businesses – Delivering Value with Speed, Integrity, and Kingdom Purpose

Movement Is Ministry When It's Done with Excellence

"Whatever you do, work at it with all your heart, as working for the Lord, not for human masters" (Colossians 3:23).

Side hustle businesses built around delivery, shipping, and courier services are more than logistical operations—they're opportunities to serve, solve problems, and build trust in your community. Whether you're transporting packages, medical specimens, or urgent documents, these ventures reflect the biblical principle of stewardship: managing what's entrusted to you with diligence and care. In a world that values speed and reliability, these businesses allow you to move with purpose, multiply income, and minister through service.

Shipping Business – Moving Goods, Building Legacy

"They will soar on wings like eagles; they will run and not grow weary..." (Isaiah 40:31).

A shipping business involves transporting goods locally, regionally, or nationally. This can range from partnering with e-commerce sellers to offering last-mile delivery for retailers. With the rise of online shopping, the demand for independent shippers has exploded. You can start with a personal vehicle, a smartphone, and a route—and grow into a fleet with contracts and recurring clients.

Startup Essentials:

- Reliable vehicle and insurance
- Route planning tools (RoadWarrior, OnFleet)
- Partnerships with platforms like Amazon Flex or ShipBob
- Branded packaging or uniforms for professionalism

This is a business of consistency and visibility—where your reputation becomes your currency.

Medical Courier Business – Delivering with Trust and Precision

"He heals the brokenhearted and binds up their wounds" (Psalm 147:3).

Medical courier services require a higher level of trust and compliance. You may be transporting lab specimens, prescriptions, medical equipment, or confidential documents. This side hustle is ideal for those who value precision, discretion, and service. It's not just about delivery—it's about protecting life and health.

Key Requirements:

- HIPAA awareness and chain-of-custody documentation
- Lockable containers and climate-controlled transport (if needed)
- Partnerships with clinics, labs, and pharmacies
- Professional appearance and punctuality

This is a ministry of healing in motion—where your reliability becomes a lifeline for others.

General Courier Business – Serving with Speed and Simplicity

"Do not withhold good from those to whom it is due, when it is in your power to act" (Proverbs 3:27).

General courier services cover a wide range of deliveries: legal documents, office supplies, retail purchases, or urgent errands. These businesses thrive on flexibility and responsiveness. You can start by offering same-day delivery in your city and expand into scheduled routes or corporate contracts.

Opportunities Include:

- Partnering with law firms, realtors, or small businesses
- Offering rush delivery or weekend service
- Advertising on Craigslist, Thumbtack, and Nextdoor
- Creating flat-rate pricing and loyalty programs

This is a business of access—where your availability becomes someone else's breakthrough.

Final Word: Deliver with Excellence, Multiply with Purpose

"The steps of a good man are ordered by the Lord..." (Psalm 37:23).

Shipping, courier, and delivery side hustles are not just about movement—they're about ministry. Every package you carry, every route you run, and every client you serve is an opportunity to reflect the excellence of the Kingdom. You're not just transporting goods—you're building trust, creating impact, and unlocking provision.

Let your business be marked by speed, integrity, and favor. Let your routes be ordered by wisdom. And let your hustle become a harvest—where service leads to overflow, and movement becomes mission.

Chapter 12: Debt Management vs. Debt Elimination – Choosing Freedom Over Financial Bondage

Stewardship Requires Strategy, But Freedom Requires Faith

"It is for freedom that Christ has set us free. Stand firm, then, and do not let yourselves be burdened again by a yoke of slavery" (Galatians 5:1).

Debt is one of the most common financial burdens believers face, yet it's often treated as a permanent fixture rather than a temporary challenge. Many settle for debt management—making minimum payments, negotiating interest rates, or consolidating balances—without realizing that God's desire is full deliverance. Debt management may offer relief, but it rarely leads to freedom. Debt elimination, on the other hand, is a bold, faith-filled pursuit of financial liberty. This chapter explores the difference between managing debt and destroying it, and how to walk in the authority God has given you to break financial yokes.

Debt Management – Survival Mode with No Exit Strategy

"The borrower is slave to the lender" (Proverbs 22:7).

Debt management is often promoted as a responsible way to handle financial obligations. It includes:

- Making minimum payments to avoid default
- Consolidating multiple debts into one loan
- Negotiating lower interest rates or extended terms
- Using hardship programs to delay payments

While these strategies can reduce stress and prevent immediate damage, they often keep you in a cycle of dependency. You're surviving, not thriving. You're maintaining the chains, not breaking them. Debt management is like putting a bandage on a spiritual wound—it may stop the bleeding, but it doesn't heal the root.

God's Word calls us to freedom, not financial captivity. Management may be a temporary tool, but it must never become a permanent mindset.

Debt Elimination – Breaking the Chains and Reclaiming Authority

"Do not owe anyone anything, except to love one another..." (Romans 13:8).

Debt elimination is the intentional, aggressive pursuit of financial freedom. It's not just about paying off balances—it's about reclaiming your power, your peace, and your purpose. It includes:

- Creating a strategic payoff plan (snowball or avalanche method)
- Cutting unnecessary expenses and redirecting funds
- Increasing income through side hustles or entrepreneurship
- Refusing to take on new debt while eliminating the old

This is spiritual warfare in the financial realm. Every payment becomes a prophetic act of deliverance. Every dollar redirected becomes a seed of restoration. Debt elimination reflects the heart of God—freedom, stewardship, and legacy.

Why Believers Must Pursue Elimination, Not Just Management

"You were bought at a price; do not become slaves of human beings" (1 Corinthians 7:23).

Debt affects more than your wallet—it affects your worship, your obedience, and your ability to walk in purpose. When you're in debt, your decisions are filtered through fear and limitation. But when you're free, you can give generously, build boldly, and respond to God's call without hesitation.

Debt management keeps you in survival mode. Debt elimination positions you for overflow. It's not just about numbers—it's about narrative. What story do you want your finances to tell?

Final Word: From Bondage to Breakthrough

"The Spirit of the Lord is upon me... to proclaim freedom for the captives and release from darkness for the prisoners" (Isaiah 61:1).

God doesn't just want you to manage your debt—He wants you to destroy it. He wants you to walk in freedom, not fear. In abundance, not anxiety. In legacy, not limitation.

Choose elimination. Choose breakthrough. Choose the path that leads to peace, prosperity, and purpose. Let your financial journey reflect the power of a God who cancels debts, restores years, and sets captives free. Let your testimony be one of victory—not just over money, but over every mindset that tried to keep you bound.

***

Section 1: Debt Management vs. Debt Elimination – Choosing Freedom Over Survival

Don't Just Manage the Chains—Break Them

"It is for freedom that Christ has set us free. Stand firm, then, and do not let yourselves be burdened again by a yoke of slavery" (Galatians 5:1).

Debt is one of the most common financial burdens in modern life, but it's also one of the most spiritually overlooked. Many believers settle for debt management—making minimum payments, juggling balances, and negotiating interest rates—without realizing that God's desire is full deliverance. Debt management is survival. Debt elimination is freedom. This chapter explores the difference between the two, and how to move from bondage to breakthrough using biblical wisdom and practical strategy.

Debt Management – Temporary Relief, Long-Term Risk

"The borrower is slave to the lender" (Proverbs 22:7).

Debt management involves controlling your debt without necessarily eliminating it. This includes:

- Consolidating loans
- Negotiating lower interest rates
- Making minimum payments to stay afloat
- Using balance transfers or hardship programs

While these tactics can provide short-term relief, they often prolong the cycle. You remain under the weight of obligation, and your financial future is tied to creditors. It's like patching a leaking roof instead of replacing it. You're managing the symptoms, not curing the condition.

God's Word doesn't call us to cope with bondage—it calls us to break it.

Debt Elimination – Breaking the Yoke Completely

"Do not owe anyone anything, except to love one another..." (Romans 13:8).

Debt elimination is the intentional, aggressive pursuit of financial freedom. It means:

- Creating a debt payoff plan (snowball or avalanche method)
- Cutting unnecessary expenses and redirecting funds
- Increasing income through side hustles or business ventures
- Refusing to take on new debt while eliminating the old

This is spiritual warfare in the financial realm. You're not just paying bills—you're reclaiming territory. Every payment becomes a prophetic act of deliverance. Every dollar redirected becomes a seed of restoration.

Debt elimination reflects the heart of God—freedom, stewardship, and legacy.

Why Believers Must Pursue Elimination, Not Just Management

"You were bought at a price; do not become slaves of human beings" (1 Corinthians 7:23).

Debt is more than a financial issue—it's a spiritual one. It affects your ability to give, to build, to invest, and to obey God's call without hesitation. When you're in debt, your decisions are filtered through fear and limitation. But when you're free, you can move with boldness and clarity.

Debt management keeps you in survival mode. Debt elimination positions you for overflow.

Final Word: From Bondage to Breakthrough

"The Spirit of the Lord is upon me... to proclaim freedom for the captives and release from darkness for the prisoners" (Isaiah 61:1).

God doesn't just want you to manage your debt—He wants you to destroy it. He wants you to walk in freedom, not fear. In abundance, not anxiety. In legacy, not limitation.

Choose elimination. Choose breakthrough. Choose the path that leads to peace, prosperity, and purpose. Let your financial journey reflect the power of a God who cancels debts, restores years, and sets captives free.

***

Section 1: When to Consolidate, When to Settle, When to Walk Away – Discerning the Path to Financial Freedom

Wisdom Knows the Season and the Strategy

"There is a time for everything, and a season for every activity under the heavens" (Ecclesiastes 3:1).

Debt can feel like a wilderness—confusing, overwhelming, and never-ending. But God has not called you to wander aimlessly. He has given you wisdom, discernment, and strategy to navigate your way out. In the journey to financial freedom, there are moments to consolidate, times to settle, and—when necessary—times to walk away. Each path requires prayer, planning, and a clear understanding of your financial landscape. This chapter will help you discern which option aligns with your current season and how to move forward with integrity and boldness.

When to Consolidate – Bringing Order to the Chaos

"Let all things be done decently and in order" (1 Corinthians 14:40).

Debt consolidation is the process of combining multiple debts into one manageable payment—often with a lower interest rate or extended term. This option is ideal when:

You have multiple high-interest debts (like credit cards or payday loans)

Your credit score is still strong enough to qualify for favorable terms

You want to simplify your payments and reduce stress

You're committed to not accumulating new debt

Consolidation is about structure. It doesn't erase the debt, but it brings clarity and control. It's a tool of stewardship—helping you manage what you owe with greater efficiency and peace.

When to Settle – Negotiating for Release

"Come now, let us settle the matter," says the Lord. "Though your sins are like scarlet, they shall be as white as snow..." (Isaiah 1:18).

Debt settlement involves negotiating with creditors to pay less than what you owe—often in a lump sum. This may be the right path when:

You're behind on payments and facing collections

Your credit score has already taken a hit

You have access to a lump sum or can save quickly

You're unable to repay the full balance but want to resolve the debt

Settlement is a form of redemption. It's not ideal for every situation, but when done ethically and strategically, it can provide a fresh start. Just as God offers grace and restoration, settlement can be a way to close a painful chapter and begin again.

When to Walk Away – Releasing What No Longer Serves You

"Forget the former things; do not dwell on the past. See, I am doing a new thing!" (Isaiah 43:18–19).

Walking away from debt—such as through bankruptcy or strategic default—is a serious decision. It may be necessary when:

You're drowning in debt with no realistic path to repay

Your income cannot sustain even minimum payments

Creditors are unwilling to negotiate or settle

You've exhausted all other options and need legal protection

This is not about irresponsibility—it's about release. Sometimes, walking away is the only way to reset. Even in scripture, debts were forgiven every seven years (Deuteronomy 15:1–2), reminding us that God values restoration over ruin. If you must walk away, do it with wisdom, legal counsel, and a plan to rebuild.

Final Word: Let the Spirit Lead Your Financial Decisions

"If any of you lacks wisdom, you should ask God, who gives generously to all without finding fault..." (James 1:5).

There is no one-size-fits-all answer when it comes to debt. What matters most is that you seek God's wisdom, understand your options, and move forward with integrity. Whether you consolidate, settle, or walk away, do it prayerfully and purposefully. Let your financial decisions reflect your faith, your growth, and your commitment to freedom.

You are not your credit score. You are not your past mistakes. You are a child of God, equipped to overcome, rebuild, and thrive. Choose the path that leads to peace, and trust that God will meet you there with provision, strategy, and grace.

***

Section 2: How to Negotiate Directly with Creditors – Speaking Boldly, Settling Wisely, and Walking in Favor

You Have the Right to Speak Up and the Authority to Be Heard

"Come now, and let us reason together, says the Lord..." (Isaiah 1:18).

Negotiating with creditors is not begging—it's advocating. It's not about shame—it's about stewardship. Many believers feel intimidated when facing debt collectors or credit card companies, but the truth is: you have more power than you think. Creditors would rather recover something than nothing, and they are often open to working with you—if you approach them with clarity, confidence, and a plan. This chapter equips you to negotiate directly with creditors, not from a place of fear, but from a place of wisdom and Kingdom authority.

Step 1: Prepare Before You Call

"Suppose one of you wants to build a tower. Won't you first sit down and estimate the cost..." (Luke 14:28).

Before you reach out to a creditor, gather all your information:

- Account numbers and balances
- Payment history and due dates
- Your current income and expenses
- A proposed payment amount or settlement offer

Know what you can realistically afford. Don't overpromise. Be ready to explain your situation clearly and calmly. Preparation is a form of honor—it shows that you're serious, responsible, and ready to resolve the matter.

Step 2: Speak with Grace and Boldness

"Let your conversation be always full of grace, seasoned with salt..." (Colossians 4:6).

When you speak to a creditor, remember: they are people too. Be respectful, but firm. Explain your hardship, your desire to resolve the debt, and your proposed solution. Ask for:

- A lower interest rate
- A reduced payoff amount (settlement)
- A payment plan with no added fees
- A "pay for delete" agreement (if negotiating collections)

Document everything. Get names, dates, and agreements in writing. Don't be afraid to ask for a supervisor if needed. You are not pleading—you are partnering to find a solution.

Step 3: Negotiate from a Position of Wisdom, Not Emotion

"The heart of the discerning acquires knowledge, for the ears of the wise seek it out" (Proverbs 18:15).

Creditors may try to pressure you into quick decisions. Don't rush. Take time to pray, review the terms, and seek counsel if needed. If the offer doesn't serve your long-term freedom, it's okay to say no. You can always call back or escalate the conversation.

Remember: you are not obligated to accept the first offer. Negotiation is a process, not a one-time event. Stay calm, stay focused, and stay grounded in truth.

Step 4: Confirm Everything in Writing

"The integrity of the upright guides them..." (Proverbs 11:3).

Never rely on verbal agreements alone. Once a settlement or payment plan is agreed upon, request a written confirmation before sending any money. This protects you from future disputes and ensures the terms are honored.

Keep copies of all letters, emails, and payment receipts. This is your paper trail of progress—and your testimony of breakthrough.

Final Word: You Are Not Powerless—You Are Positioned

"You will also decree a thing, and it will be established for you..." (Job 22:28).

Negotiating with creditors is not just a financial act—it's a spiritual one. It's declaring, "I will not be bound by fear. I will not be buried by debt. I will walk in wisdom, favor, and freedom." You are not at the mercy of the system—you are a child of God, equipped with strategy and covered in grace.

Speak up. Stand firm. And settle with confidence. What the enemy meant to use as a yoke, God will use as a testimony. Let your negotiation be a declaration: "I am not defeated—I am delivered."

Chapter 13: Building Legacy Through Financial Literacy – Empowering Generations with Wisdom and Wealth

Legacy Begins with Knowledge and Ends in Impact

"A good person leaves an inheritance for their children's children..." (Proverbs 13:22).

Legacy is more than money—it's mindset. It's not just what you leave behind, but what you build into others while you're here. Financial literacy is the foundation of legacy because it equips you to steward resources wisely, break generational cycles of lack, and empower your family to walk in abundance. When you understand how money works—how to earn, manage, multiply, and protect it—you're not just surviving, you're sowing. You're planting seeds of wisdom that will bear fruit for generations.

Financial Literacy Is a Form of Discipleship

"My people are destroyed for lack of knowledge..." (Hosea 4:6).

Many believers struggle financially not because they lack faith, but because they lack financial understanding. They tithe faithfully but overspend. They give generously but borrow recklessly. Financial literacy bridges the gap between spiritual conviction and practical application. It teaches budgeting, saving, investing, and debt elimination—not as worldly strategies, but as Kingdom principles of stewardship.

Teaching your children, your community, or your congregation how to handle money is a form of discipleship. It's equipping them to walk in wisdom, avoid traps, and build wealth that honors God.

Breaking Cycles and Building Systems

"The wise store up choice food and olive oil, but fools gulp theirs down" (Proverbs 21:20).

Financial literacy helps you recognize patterns—both healthy and harmful. It exposes the traps of payday loans, credit card debt, and impulse spending. It teaches you how to build systems: automatic savings, emergency funds, investment portfolios, and debt payoff plans. These systems create stability, and stability creates legacy.

When you break cycles of financial dysfunction, you don't just change your life—you change your lineage. You become the pivot point. The curse breaker. The blueprint builder.

Teaching Financial Literacy Is a Kingdom Assignment

"Train up a child in the way he should go, and when he is old he will not depart from it" (Proverbs 22:6).

Whether you're a parent, pastor, educator, or entrepreneur, teaching financial literacy is part of your Kingdom assignment. It's not just about money—it's about mission. When people are financially free, they can give more, serve more, and dream bigger. They can fund ministries, launch businesses, and leave inheritances.

You don't need a finance degree to teach financial literacy—you need a testimony, a strategy, and a willingness to share. Every budget you build, every debt you destroy, and every investment you make becomes a lesson for someone else.

Final Word: Build What Outlives You

"Unless the Lord builds the house, the builders labor in vain..." (Psalm 127:1).

Financial literacy is the tool. Legacy is the outcome. When you build with wisdom, you build something that outlives you. You create a ripple effect of empowerment, stewardship, and prosperity. You leave behind more than assets—you leave behind answers.

Let your legacy be marked by clarity, courage, and conviction. Teach what you've learned. Share what you've overcome. And build systems that speak long after you're gone. Because when you build with God, your legacy becomes eternal.

***

Section 1: Teaching Your Children and Community – Multiplying Wisdom, Breaking Cycles, and Building Kingdom Legacy

Financial Wisdom Is Meant to Be Shared

"These commandments that I give you today are to be on your hearts. Impress them on your children. Talk about them when you sit at home and when you walk along the road..." (Deuteronomy 6:6–7).

Financial literacy is not just a personal breakthrough—it's a generational assignment. When you learn how to steward money, manage debt, build wealth, and walk in financial integrity, you carry a responsibility to teach others. Your children, your community, and your church need what you've learned. Teaching financial principles is a form of discipleship. It's how we multiply wisdom, break generational curses, and build Kingdom legacy. This chapter explores how to pass on financial truth with clarity, compassion, and conviction.

Start with Your Children – Build Early, Build Strong

"Train up a child in the way he should go, and when he is old he will not depart from it" (Proverbs 22:6).

Children are sponges. They absorb what we model more than what we say. Teaching them about money—how to earn it, save it, give it, and grow it—is one of the most powerful gifts you can give. Start with simple lessons:

- Let them earn money through chores or creative projects
- Teach them to tithe and give generously
- Help them set savings goals and track progress
- Talk openly about budgeting and wise spending

These lessons become seeds. And when planted early, they produce fruit that lasts a lifetime.

Equip Your Community – Turn Your Testimony into a Toolkit

"Let the redeemed of the Lord tell their story..." (Psalm 107:2).

Your financial journey—whether marked by struggle, breakthrough, or both—is a testimony. Don't hide it. Use it. Host workshops, write guides, lead small groups, or mentor others one-on-one. Share what you've learned about credit, debt, budgeting, and entrepreneurship. Use scripture to anchor every principle, and practical tools to make it actionable.

When you teach your community, you're not just giving information—you're giving transformation. You're empowering others to walk in freedom, dignity, and purpose.

Break Cycles and Build Systems

"The wise store up knowledge..." (Proverbs 10:14).

Many families and communities are trapped in cycles of financial dysfunction—poverty, overspending, fear, and lack. Teaching financial literacy breaks those cycles. It replaces confusion with clarity, and chaos with strategy. Help others build systems:

- Monthly budgets
- Emergency funds
- Debt payoff plans
- Side hustle strategies
- Investment basics

These systems become scaffolding for legacy. They create stability, and stability creates opportunity.

Final Word: Multiply What God Has Given You

"You have been faithful with a few things; I will put you in charge of many things..." (Matthew 25:23).

Teaching financial literacy is not about perfection—it's about multiplication. You don't need to be a financial expert. You just need to be faithful. Share what you know. Model what you live. And speak life into those who are still learning.

Let your children rise with wisdom. Let your community walk in freedom. And let your legacy be marked by multiplication—where what God taught you becomes a blessing for generations to come. You are not just a student—you are a steward. And your classroom is everywhere you go.

***

Section 2: Creating Generational Wealth Through Credit, Ownership, and Stewardship – Building What Lasts Beyond You

Wealth Is Not Just Accumulated—It's Assigned

"The wealth of the sinner is stored up for the righteous" (Proverbs 13:22).

Generational wealth is more than passing down money—it's passing down mindsets, systems, and spiritual authority. It's the intentional creation of resources that outlive you and empower your descendants to walk in purpose, not just provision. In the Kingdom, wealth is not just about accumulation—it's about assignment. God gives us tools like credit, ownership, and stewardship to build legacy, influence culture, and fund Kingdom work. This chapter explores how to use these tools wisely to create generational wealth that reflects both excellence and obedience.

Credit – Leveraging Access Without Becoming a Slave

"The borrower is slave to the lender" (Proverbs 22:7).

Credit, when used wisely, is a tool—not a trap. It can open doors to real estate, business funding, and strategic investments. But when misused, it becomes bondage. Generational wealth requires understanding how to build and protect credit:

- Maintain low balances and pay on time
- Use credit to acquire assets, not liabilities
- Monitor your reports and dispute errors
- Teach your children how credit works before they need it

Credit is access. But access must be governed by wisdom. When you master credit, you model financial authority—not just for yourself, but for your lineage.

Ownership – Possessing What Produces

"You will be blessed in the land the Lord your God is giving you" (Deuteronomy 28:8).

Ownership is a cornerstone of generational wealth. Whether it's land, homes, businesses, or intellectual property, what you own can multiply beyond your lifetime. Ownership creates stability, equity, and inheritance. It allows you to:

- Build passive income through rental properties or royalties
- Transfer assets to your children tax-efficiently
- Create businesses that employ and empower others
- Protect your family from displacement and poverty

God is a God of territory. He gives land, influence, and dominion. Ownership is not just financial—it's prophetic. It declares, "This belongs to me and my children's children."

Stewardship – Managing What Multiplies

"Who then is the faithful and wise steward...?" (Luke 12:42).

Stewardship is the spiritual foundation of wealth. It's not just about what you have—it's about how you manage it. Generational wealth requires systems, discipline, and vision. Stewardship includes:

- Budgeting and saving consistently
- Investing with long-term strategy
- Giving generously and strategically
- Teaching financial literacy to your family and community

Stewardship turns income into impact. It transforms resources into legacy. It's the difference between having money and multiplying mission.

Final Word: Build What Heaven Can Bless

"Unless the Lord builds the house, the builders labor in vain..." (Psalm 127:1).

Generational wealth is not just a financial goal—it's a Kingdom assignment. It's about building what heaven can bless and your descendants can inherit. Use credit with wisdom. Pursue ownership with boldness. Steward resources with faithfulness. And teach others to do the same.

Let your legacy be marked by clarity, courage, and covenant. You are not just building wealth—you are building testimony. You are not just acquiring assets—you are activating inheritance. And what you build today will echo in eternity.

***

Section 3: Prophetic Declarations for Financial Restoration – Speaking Life Over Lack and Calling Forth Breakthrough

Your Words Create Atmosphere and Activate Authority

"Death and life are in the power of the tongue, and those who love it will eat its fruit" (Proverbs 18:21).

Financial restoration begins with revelation—but it is sustained by declaration. In the Kingdom of God, we don't just react to circumstances—we speak to them. Prophetic declarations are not empty affirmations; they are Spirit-led proclamations that align your mouth with God's promises. When you declare restoration over your finances, you are not denying reality—you are commanding it to shift. This chapter equips you to speak boldly, believe deeply, and decree breakthrough with scriptural authority.

Declare What God Has Already Promised

"You will also decree a thing, and it will be established for you; and light will shine on your ways" (Job 22:28).

God has already spoken abundance, provision, and restoration over His people. Your role is to echo His Word. Prophetic declarations are not wishful thinking—they are legal transactions in the spirit realm. When you speak what God has said, Heaven backs your words.

Examples:

- "I declare that I am the head and not the tail, above only and never beneath" (Deuteronomy 28:13).
- "I declare that wealth and riches are in my house, and my righteousness endures forever" (Psalm 112:3).
- "I declare that the devourer is rebuked, and my harvest is protected" (Malachi 3:11).

These are not just verses—they are verdicts. Speak them with faith, and expect manifestation.

Break the Spirit of Poverty with Prophetic Fire

"The Lord will open the heavens, the storehouse of His bounty... to bless all the work of your hands" (Deuteronomy 28:12).

Poverty is not just a financial condition—it's a spiritual stronghold. It whispers lies of limitation, scarcity, and shame. But prophetic declarations break its grip. When you speak restoration, you dismantle the enemy's narrative and replace it with God's truth.

Declare:

- "I break every generational curse of financial lack and declare supernatural increase."
- "I cancel every assignment of debt, delay, and denial over my finances."
- "I release divine strategies, favor, and open doors for wealth creation."

Your voice is a weapon. Use it to tear down what was never meant to stand.

Call Forth What's Been Held Back

"The thief comes only to steal and kill and destroy; I have come that they may have life, and have it to the full" (John 10:10).

Sometimes restoration means reclaiming what was stolen—time, money, opportunities, or inheritance. Prophetic declarations call forth what's been delayed, denied, or diverted. You are not begging—you are enforcing spiritual justice.

Declare:

- "I command every stolen opportunity to be returned sevenfold" (Proverbs 6:31).
- "I speak resurrection over dormant dreams and buried businesses."
- "I declare that contracts, clients, and capital are locating me now."

Restoration is not passive—it's prophetic. Speak it until you see it.

Final Word: Speak Until You See the Shift

"Let the redeemed of the Lord say so..." (Psalm 107:2).

Your financial restoration is not just a hope—it's a harvest. And your declarations are the seeds. Speak daily. Speak boldly. Speak with scripture as your sword and faith as your fire. Don't wait for the breakthrough to speak—speak until the breakthrough comes.

Let your mouth become a mantle. Let your words become weapons. And let your declarations become the doorway to divine provision. You are not just recovering—you are rising. You are not just rebuilding—you are reigning. Speak life. Speak legacy. Speak restoration.

Bonus Section: The 1% Playbook – Sample Dispute Letters and the Power of Strategic Advocacy

The Righteous Must Know How to Speak and Write with Authority

"Open your mouth for the mute, for the rights of all who are destitute. Open your mouth, judge righteously, defend the rights of the poor and needy" (Proverbs 31:8–9).

In the realm of financial restoration, one of the most overlooked weapons is the written word. Dispute letters are not just administrative tools—they are strategic declarations that challenge error, demand accountability, and protect your financial identity. The "1% Playbook" refers to the high-level strategies used by the financially elite to correct inaccuracies, negotiate terms, and reclaim what's rightfully theirs. As Kingdom citizens, we must learn to do the same—not with arrogance, but with clarity, boldness, and truth. This section provides sample dispute letter frameworks and biblical insight into why written advocacy matters.

Why Dispute Letters Matter

"Write the vision and make it plain on tablets, so he may run who reads it" (Habakkuk 2:2).

Dispute letters are your written defense against inaccurate credit reporting, unfair collections, and unauthorized charges. They serve as legal documentation, spiritual resistance, and practical correction. When you write a dispute letter, you're not just asking for change—you're commanding it. You're holding institutions accountable and protecting your name, which is part of your legacy.

Whether you're challenging a debt, requesting validation, or demanding removal of erroneous information, your words must be clear, firm, and rooted in truth.

Sample Dispute Letter Framework: Credit Report Error

Subject: Request for Investigation of Inaccurate Information **To**: [Credit Bureau Name] **Date**: [Insert Date]

Dear [Credit Bureau],

I am writing to formally dispute the following item on my credit report. The account listed under [Creditor Name] with account number [XXXX] is inaccurate. I am requesting an immediate investigation and removal of this item under the Fair Credit Reporting Act (FCRA).

Please find enclosed documentation supporting my claim, including [list documents]. I request that this item be corrected or deleted within 30 days, as required by law.

Thank you for your prompt attention to this matter.

Sincerely, [Your Full Name] [Your Address] [Your Date of Birth] [Your Social Security Number (last 4 digits)]

Sample Dispute Letter Framework: Debt Validation Request

Subject: Request for Debt Validation **To**: [Debt Collector Name] **Date**: [Insert Date]

Dear [Debt Collector],

This letter is in response to your recent communication regarding an alleged debt. Under the Fair Debt Collection Practices Act (FDCPA), I am requesting validation of this debt. Please provide the following:

- Proof that I owe the debt
- A copy of the original contract or agreement
- The name and address of the original creditor
- A breakdown of the amount claimed

Until this information is provided, I request that all collection activity cease. I also request that this debt not be reported to any credit bureau until validation is complete.

Sincerely, [Your Full Name] [Your Address]

Biblical Advocacy Through Written Strategy

"Let your conversation be always full of grace, seasoned with salt, so that you may know how to answer everyone" (Colossians 4:6).

Writing dispute letters is not just about financial correction—it's about spiritual advocacy. You are defending what God has entrusted to you. You are protecting your name, your credit, and your capacity to build legacy. Just as Nehemiah wrote letters to secure safe passage and resources for rebuilding (Nehemiah 2:7–8), you too must write with purpose and precision.

Final Word: Write It, Send It, Stand on It

"No weapon formed against you shall prosper, and every tongue which rises against you in judgment you shall condemn..." (Isaiah 54:17).

Dispute letters are part of your financial warfare. They are written decrees that challenge injustice and activate restoration. Don't delay. Don't doubt. Write with clarity. Send with confidence. And stand on the Word of God as your foundation.

Let your letters be strategic. Let your tone be righteous. And let your results be undeniable. You are not just correcting a report—you are reclaiming your financial identity and restoring your legacy.

***

2. Credit Repair Checklist – Rebuilding Your Name, Restoring Your Narrative

Your Credit Is a Tool, Not Your Identity

"A good name is more desirable than great riches; to be esteemed is better than silver or gold" (Proverbs 22:1).

Credit is not just a number—it's a reflection of your financial habits, your history, and your ability to access opportunity. But even if your credit has been damaged by hardship, delay, or lack of knowledge, restoration is possible. God is a restorer, and that includes your financial reputation. This chapter provides a step-by-step credit repair checklist to help you rebuild with wisdom, integrity, and strategy. You are not disqualified—you are being equipped.

Step 1: Pull Your Credit Reports

"The prudent see danger and take refuge, but the simple keep going and pay the penalty" (Proverbs 27:12).

Start by requesting your credit reports from all three major bureaus—Equifax, Experian, and TransUnion—at AnnualCreditReport.com. Review each report line by line. Look for:

- Inaccurate personal information
- Duplicate accounts
- Late payments you didn't make
- Accounts that don't belong to you
- Collections that should have aged off

You can't fix what you don't face. This is your financial inventory—treat it like a spiritual audit.

Step 2: Dispute Inaccuracies

"Speak up and judge fairly; defend the rights of the poor and needy" (Proverbs 31:9).

If you find errors, file disputes with each credit bureau. Use certified mail and keep copies of all correspondence. Include:

- A clear explanation of the error
- Supporting documentation (if available)
- A request for correction or deletion

This is your right under the Fair Credit Reporting Act (FCRA). You are not begging—you are advocating. And when you advocate with truth, Heaven backs you.

Step 3: Pay Down Revolving Balances

"The wicked borrow and do not repay, but the righteous give generously" (Psalm 37:21).

Your credit utilization ratio—how much of your available credit you're using—makes up a significant portion of your score. Aim to keep balances below 30%, and ideally under 10%. Start by paying down the smallest balances first or focus on the highest interest rates.

This isn't just about numbers—it's about integrity. Paying what you owe, even in small steps, is a form of worship and witness.

Step 4: Negotiate and Settle Debts Strategically

"Settle matters quickly with your adversary..." (Matthew 5:25).

If you have collections or charged-off accounts, consider negotiating a settlement. Ask for a "pay for delete" agreement in writing before sending payment. If they won't delete, request that the account be marked "paid in full" or "settled."

This is about closing doors to the past so you can walk freely into your future. Don't let old debts keep you from new opportunities.

Step 5: Build Positive Credit History

"Whoever can be trusted with very little can also be trusted with much..." (Luke 16:10).

Once you've cleaned up your report, it's time to rebuild. Consider:

- Secured credit cards
- Credit-builder loans
- Becoming an authorized user on a trusted account
- Paying all bills on time, every time

Consistency is key. Every on-time payment is a seed. Every wise decision is a brick in your financial foundation.

Final Word: Restoration Is Your Portion

"I will restore to you the years that the swarming locust has eaten..." (Joel 2:25).

Credit repair is not just about numbers—it's about narrative. It's about rewriting the story the enemy tried to use against you. With diligence, prayer, and strategy, you can rebuild your credit, reclaim your name, and walk in financial favor.

Let this checklist be your roadmap. Let the Word be your anchor. And let your testimony be this: "I was once denied, but now I'm approved. I was once overlooked, but now I'm trusted. I was once broken, but now I'm restored."

***

3. Bonus Section: Auction Bidding Cheat Sheet – Winning with Wisdom, Strategy, and Stewardship

You Don't Just Bid with Money—You Bid with Discernment

"The plans of the diligent lead surely to abundance, but everyone who is hasty comes only to poverty" (Proverbs 21:5).

Auction bidding—whether for vehicles, real estate, surplus inventory, or seized assets—is a powerful way to acquire value at a fraction of the cost. But it's not just about showing up and raising your paddle. It's about strategy, timing, and spiritual discernment. In the Kingdom, we don't chase deals—we steward opportunities. This cheat sheet equips you to bid with clarity, avoid emotional traps, and walk away with assets that multiply your mission.

Know What You're Bidding On

"The wise store up knowledge, but the mouth of a fool invites ruin" (Proverbs 10:14).

Before you bid, research the item thoroughly. Whether it's a car, a property, or a pallet of electronics, know:

Its market value

Its condition (request inspection reports if available)

Any hidden fees (buyer's premium, taxes, transport)

The auction terms (reserve price, payment deadlines, refund policy)

Don't bid blindly. Wisdom begins with information. The more you know, the more confidently you can move.

Set Your Maximum Bid Before You Enter

"Like a city whose walls are broken through is a person who lacks self-control" (Proverbs 25:28).

Auctions are emotional environments. The adrenaline, competition, and urgency can tempt you to overspend. That's why you must set your maximum bid in advance—and stick to it. Decide:

What you're willing to pay

What profit margin you need (if reselling)

What your walk-away point is

This is not just financial discipline—it's spiritual self-control. You're not there to win every bid. You're there to win the right one.

Watch the Flow Before You Jump In

"Be quick to listen, slow to speak..." (James 1:19).

Whether it's a live auction or an online platform, observe the bidding rhythm before participating. Watch how fast bids rise, who's bidding aggressively, and how the auctioneer operates. This gives you insight into timing and strategy.

Sometimes the best move is to wait until the final seconds. Other times, an early bid can signal strength and deter competition. Let discernment guide your pace.

Bid with Boldness, Exit with Peace

"Let the peace of Christ rule in your hearts..." (Colossians 3:15).

When it's time to bid, do so with confidence. Don't second-guess. Don't chase. If you win, celebrate with gratitude. If you lose, walk away with peace. God's favor isn't limited to one auction. What's for you cannot be taken from you.

Remember: every bid is a seed. Sow it wisely. Reap it joyfully. And let your stewardship speak louder than your spending.

Final Word: Steward the Win, Don't Worship It

"Command them to do good, to be rich in good deeds, and to be generous and willing to share" (1 Timothy 6:18).

Winning an auction is just the beginning. What matters most is how you use what you've acquired. Whether it's for resale, personal use, or Kingdom expansion, let your assets serve a purpose greater than profit. Steward the win. Multiply the impact. And never let the pursuit of deals distract you from the pursuit of destiny.

Let your bids be strategic. Let your wins be fruitful. And let your heart remain anchored in wisdom, not wealth.

***

4. Loan Application Scripts – Speaking with Confidence, Clarity, and Covenant Authority

Your Voice Is a Vessel of Favor

"Let your conversation be always full of grace, seasoned with salt, so that you may know how to answer everyone" (Colossians 4:6).

Applying for a loan—whether for a home, business, vehicle, or personal need—can feel intimidating. But as a Kingdom builder, you are not approaching lenders as a beggar. You are approaching as a steward, a visionary, and a covenant carrier. The words you speak during a loan application matter. They shape perception, build trust, and open doors. This chapter equips you with loan application scripts that reflect professionalism, wisdom, and spiritual confidence—so you can advocate for your vision with clarity and favor.

Script for Business Loan Application

"Commit to the Lord whatever you do, and He will establish your plans" (Proverbs 16:3).

Opening Statement: "Thank you for taking the time to meet with me. I'm applying for a business loan to expand [Business Name], which serves [target audience] with [product/service]. Our mission is rooted in excellence, community impact, and sustainable growth. I've prepared a detailed business plan, financial projections, and documentation to support this request."

Key Phrases to Include:

- "We've experienced consistent growth and are now positioned to scale."
- "This funding will allow us to [hire staff, purchase equipment, expand marketing, etc.]."
- "We're committed to responsible repayment and long-term partnership."

Closing Declaration: "I believe this investment will not only yield financial return but also community transformation. I'm confident in the vision, and I'm prepared to steward this opportunity with integrity."

Script for Personal Loan Application

"The Lord will guide you always; He will satisfy your needs in a sun-scorched land..." (Isaiah 58:11).

Opening Statement: "I'm applying for a personal loan to consolidate debt and stabilize my financial foundation. I've taken proactive steps to manage my budget, reduce expenses, and increase income through side hustles and freelance work."

Key Phrases to Include:

- "This loan will allow me to simplify payments and reduce interest."
- "I've maintained consistent employment and have a clear repayment plan."
- "I'm committed to financial restoration and long-term stewardship."

Closing Declaration: "I'm not just seeking relief—I'm pursuing restoration. This loan is part of a larger strategy to walk in financial freedom and honor every obligation."

Script for Mortgage or Vehicle Loan Application

"You will be blessed when you come in and blessed when you go out" (Deuteronomy 28:6).

Opening Statement: "I'm applying for a [mortgage/vehicle] loan to secure a stable foundation for my family and future. I've prepared all necessary documentation, including income verification, credit history, and down payment details."

Key Phrases to Include:

- "This purchase aligns with my long-term financial goals."
- "I've budgeted carefully to ensure affordability and sustainability."
- "I'm seeking a fair interest rate and terms that reflect my financial discipline."

Closing Declaration: "This isn't just a transaction—it's a step toward legacy. I'm committed to honoring this agreement and building with wisdom."

Final Word: Speak as a Steward, Not a Slave

"You will also decree a thing, and it will be established for you..." (Job 22:28).

Your loan application is not just a financial request—it's a prophetic moment. Speak with clarity. Present with excellence. And declare with faith. You are not just asking—you are activating. You are not just applying—you are aligning. Let your words reflect your vision, your values, and your victory.

Whether you're building a business, buying a home, or restoring your finances, speak as one who carries favor. Because when Heaven backs your voice, doors open that no man can shut.

***

5. Tradeline Tracker – Monitoring Your Credit Growth with Wisdom and Intentionality

What You Track, You Can Transform

"Know well the condition of your flocks, and give attention to your herds; for riches do not last forever..." (Proverbs 27:23–24).

In the journey of financial restoration, one of the most powerful tools you can use is a tradeline tracker. Tradelines are the accounts listed on your credit report—credit cards, loans, mortgages, and lines of credit. Tracking these accounts helps you monitor your credit health, identify opportunities for growth, and catch errors before they become obstacles. Just as a shepherd watches over their flock, you must watch over your financial profile with diligence and discernment. A tradeline tracker is not just a spreadsheet—it's a strategy.

Why Tradeline Tracking Matters

"The wise store up knowledge, but the mouth of a fool invites ruin" (Proverbs 10:14).

Every tradeline impacts your credit score differently. Some build history, others carry risk. By tracking your tradelines, you gain insight into:

- Payment history and due dates
- Credit utilization ratios
- Account age and status
- Potential errors or fraudulent activity

This awareness empowers you to make informed decisions. You can prioritize which accounts to pay down, which ones to close, and which ones to leverage for credit building. Tradeline tracking turns confusion into clarity—and clarity into breakthrough.

What to Include in Your Tradeline Tracker

"Let all things be done decently and in order" (1 Corinthians 14:40).

Your tradeline tracker should be simple, consistent, and updated monthly. Include columns for:

- Creditor name and account number (last 4 digits)
- Type of account (credit card, loan, etc.)
- Opening date and current balance
- Credit limit and utilization percentage
- Payment due date and status (on-time, late, deferred)
- Notes (disputes, settlements, goals)

This system helps you steward your credit with excellence. It's not just about numbers—it's about narrative. You're writing a new financial story, one account at a time.

Using Your Tracker to Build Strategy

"Plans fail for lack of counsel, but with many advisers they succeed" (Proverbs 15:22).

Once your tradeline tracker is in place, use it to set goals:

- Pay down high-utilization accounts first
- Keep older accounts open to preserve credit age
- Avoid unnecessary inquiries or new accounts
- Monitor for changes in reporting or suspicious activity

You can also use your tracker to prepare for major financial moves—like applying for a mortgage, business loan, or credit card. Lenders will see what you've already stewarded, and favor will follow your faithfulness.

Final Word: Track It, Tame It, Transform It

"The steps of a good man are ordered by the Lord..." (Psalm 37:23).

Your tradeline tracker is more than a tool—it's a testimony. It shows that you're not just reacting to your finances—you're ruling over them. You're not just surviving—you're stewarding. And as you track your credit growth with wisdom, you'll see restoration unfold in real time.

Let your tracker be a reflection of your diligence. Let your diligence be a reflection of your faith. And let your faith lead you into financial freedom, one tradeline at a time.

***

6. Monthly Credit Score Planner – Building Consistency, Tracking Progress, and Stewarding Your Financial Reputation

Restoration Requires Rhythm, Not Just Revelation

"Teach us to number our days, that we may gain a heart of wisdom" (Psalm 90:12).

Your credit score is not just a number—it's a reflection of your financial stewardship, consistency, and credibility. And like any area of restoration, breakthrough comes through rhythm. A monthly credit score planner helps you track your progress, set intentional goals, and stay accountable to the vision God has given you for financial freedom. This isn't just about improving your score—it's about building a testimony of diligence, wisdom, and favor.

Why You Need a Monthly Planner

"The plans of the diligent lead surely to abundance..." (Proverbs 21:5).

Credit scores fluctuate based on payment history, credit utilization, account age, inquiries, and derogatory marks. Without a system to monitor these factors, it's easy to miss opportunities for growth or overlook errors that sabotage your progress. A monthly planner helps you:

- Track your score across all three bureaus
- Monitor changes in balances and utilization
- Record payment dates and dispute activity
- Set monthly goals for debt reduction or credit building

This planner becomes your financial dashboard—a tool of clarity and control.

What to Include in Your Monthly Credit Score Planner

"Let all things be done decently and in order" (1 Corinthians 14:40).

Your planner should be simple, strategic, and Spirit-led. Include sections for:

- **Current credit scores** (Equifax, Experian, TransUnion)

- **Total debt owed** and **monthly payments made**
- **Credit utilization percentage** per account
- **New inquiries or accounts opened**
- **Disputes filed or resolved**
- **Goals for the month** (e.g., "Pay off $300 on Capital One," "Dispute late payment on medical bill")

This structure helps you steward your financial reputation with excellence. You're not just reacting—you're ruling.

Using the Planner to Build Momentum

"Write the vision and make it plain..." (Habakkuk 2:2).

Each month, review your progress and adjust your strategy. Celebrate small wins—like a 10-point score increase or a paid-off account. Document setbacks and learn from them. Use the planner to pray over your finances, declare restoration, and stay focused on your long-term goals.

Momentum is built through movement. And movement requires measurement. Your planner becomes a prophetic tool—tracking the fruit of your faith and the evidence of your diligence.

Final Word: Steward Your Score, Strengthen Your Story

"The integrity of the upright guides them..." (Proverbs 11:3).

Your credit score is part of your financial witness. It opens doors to housing, business funding, and generational wealth. But more than that, it reflects your journey of restoration. With a monthly planner, you move from confusion to clarity, from reaction to strategy, and from survival to stewardship.

Let this planner be your altar of accountability. Let each entry be a seed of breakthrough. And let your score rise as your story unfolds—one month, one step, one act of faith at a time.

Prayer for Financial Healing

Closing Chapter: Faith + Strategy = Breakthrough

Faith Is the Foundation, Strategy Is the Blueprint, Breakthrough Is the Promise

"The Lord will guide you always; He will satisfy your needs in a sun-scorched land and will strengthen your frame. You will be like a well-watered garden, like a spring whose waters never fail" (Isaiah 58:11).

As we close this journey of financial restoration, we declare that breakthrough is not just possible—it is promised. When faith and strategy walk hand in hand, mountains move, debts dissolve, and legacies are born. You are not just rebuilding your finances—you are reclaiming your authority, rewriting your story, and restoring what the enemy tried to steal. Let this final chapter be your altar of surrender and your launching pad of victory.

Prayer for Financial Healing

Heavenly Father, I come before You with a heart open to healing, restoration, and divine strategy. You are Jehovah Jireh—my Provider—and I trust You to meet every need according to Your riches in glory (Philippians 4:19). I repent for any mismanagement, fear, or agreement with lack, and I receive Your grace to start anew.

Lord, heal the wounds caused by financial trauma. Break every generational curse of poverty, debt, and delay. Uproot every lie that says I am not worthy of abundance. Silence every voice of shame, and replace it with Your truth: that I am chosen, equipped, and empowered to prosper.

Give me wisdom to steward what I have. Give me strategy to multiply what I earn. Give me favor to access what I need. Let doors open that no man can shut. Let resources flow from unexpected places. Let my finances reflect Your glory and my life reflect Your goodness.

I declare that I am walking into overflow. I declare that I am debt-free, fear-free, and future-focused. I declare that my hands are blessed, my mind is clear, and my path is ordered by You.

Thank You for being my source, my shield, and my solution. I receive Your healing, Your help, and Your harvest. In Jesus' name, Amen.

Final Word: You are not just a reader—you are a rebuilder. You are not just a borrower—you are a breaker of chains. You are not just surviving—you are stepping into supernatural strategy. Let faith lead. Let wisdom guide. And let breakthrough be your portion.

Now go forth and build—because your legacy begins today.

***

Prophetic Prayer of Decrees: Restoration, Ownership, and Favor

Heavenly Father, In the mighty name of Jesus, I come boldly before Your throne—not as a beggar, but as a blood-bought heir of the Kingdom. I stand in the authority of Your Word and decree divine restoration, supernatural ownership, and uncommon favor over every area of my life.

Restoration

I decree that everything stolen, delayed, or destroyed in my finances, family, and future is being restored sevenfold according to Proverbs 6:31. I call back lost time, missed opportunities, and squandered resources. I declare Joel 2:25 over my life: *"I will restore to you the years that the locust has eaten."* Let every dry place become a well-watered garden. Let every broken place be rebuilt stronger. Let every closed door swing open by the hand of the Lord.

Ownership

I decree that I am stepping into ownership—of land, homes, businesses, and intellectual property. I declare Deuteronomy 28:11–12: *"The Lord will grant you abundant prosperity... The Lord will open the heavens... to bless all the work of your hands."* I will no longer rent what I am called to rule. I will no longer borrow what I am anointed to build. I receive deeds, titles, contracts, and keys in Jesus' name. I am a lender, not a borrower. I am an owner, not a wanderer. I possess what God has promised.

Favor

I decree that divine favor surrounds me like a shield (Psalm 5:12). I walk into rooms where my name has already been spoken with honor. I receive favor with lenders, investors, clients, and gatekeepers. I declare Luke 2:52 over my life: *"And Jesus grew in wisdom and stature, and in favor with God and man."* Let favor accelerate what labor could never earn. Let favor open doors that credentials cannot. Let favor distinguish me in every space I enter.

Father, I seal these decrees in the blood of Jesus. I cancel every demonic delay, every generational curse, and every lie of lack. I rise in faith, I move in strategy, and I walk in victory. What You have spoken, I will see. What You have promised, I will possess.

In Jesus' mighty name, **Amen and Amen.**

Now declare it aloud: "This is my season of restoration. This is my season of ownership. This is my season of favor."

***

Final Charge Prayer: Rise, Rebuild, and Reign

Heavenly Father, In the name of Jesus, I step into this moment with holy boldness and prophetic fire. I thank You for every lesson, every battle, and every breakthrough that has brought me to this threshold. I declare that I am no longer bound by fear, delay, or defeat—I am rising, rebuilding, and reigning by the power of Your Spirit.

Rise

I decree that I rise from the ashes of financial ruin, emotional exhaustion, and spiritual stagnation. I rise with renewed strength, divine clarity, and supernatural courage. I declare Isaiah 60:1 over my life: *"Arise, shine, for your light has come, and the glory of the Lord rises upon you."* I rise above every generational curse, every limiting belief, and every demonic assignment. I rise into purpose, into power, and into prophetic positioning.

Rebuild

I decree that I rebuild what was torn down—my finances, my faith, my family, and my future. I declare Nehemiah 2:20: *"The God of heaven will give us success. We His servants will start rebuilding."* I rebuild with strategy, with excellence, and with divine blueprints. I lay foundations of righteousness, wisdom, and legacy. I rebuild businesses, ministries, and movements that reflect Your glory and expand Your Kingdom.

Reign

I decree that I reign in life through Christ Jesus (Romans 5:17). I reign over debt, over delay, over distraction, and over defeat. I reign with integrity, with influence, and with divine authority. I declare that I am seated in heavenly places, crowned with favor, and clothed in strength. I reign not for vanity, but for victory—not for status, but for service.

Father, I receive this charge. I embrace this mantle. I walk in this anointing. Let every step I take be ordered by You. Let every word I speak carry weight. Let every seed I sow produce harvest. I will not shrink back. I will not settle. I will not surrender. I rise. I rebuild. I reign. In Jesus' mighty name, **Amen and Amen.**

Declare it aloud: "I rise with power. I rebuild with purpose. I reign with favor. This is my charge, and I will fulfill it."

About the Publisher

Keshia Davis is a visionary author, spiritual strategist, and publisher dedicated to empowering believers through biblically grounded, spiritually intense resources. With a passion for deliverance, healing, and divine purpose, she creates prayer manuals and devotional tools that equip readers to walk in freedom, authority, and truth.

www.ingramcontent.com/pod-product-compliance
Lightning Source LLC
LaVergne TN
LVHW090310210926
848480LV00001B/196